HELEN PREJEAN

People of God

Remarkable Lives, Heroes of Faith

People of God is a series of inspiring biographies for the general reader. Each volume offers a compelling and honest narrative of the life of an important twentieth- or twenty-first-century Catholic. Some living and some now deceased, each of these women and men has known challenges and weaknesses familiar to most of us but responded to them in ways that call us to our own forms of heroism. Each offers a credible and concrete witness of faith, hope, and love to people of our own day.

John XXIII	Massimo Faggioli
Oscar Romero	Kevin Clarke
Thomas Merton	Michael W. Higgins
Francis	Michael Collins
Flannery O'Connor	Angela O'Donnell
Martin Sheen	Rose Pacatte
Jean Vanier	Michael W. Higgins
Dorothy Day	Patrick Jordan
Luis Antonio Tagle	Cindy Wooden
Georges and Pauline Vanier	Mary Francis Coady
Joseph Bernardin	Steven P. Millies
Corita Kent	Rose Pacatte
Daniel Rudd	Gary B. Agee
Helen Prejean	Joyce Duriga
Paul VI	Michael Collins
Elizabeth Johnson	Heidi Schlumpf
Thea Bowman	Maurice J. Nutt
Shahbaz Bhatti	John L. Allen Jr.

More titles to follow. . . .

Helen Prejean

Death Row's Nun

Joyce Duriga

LITURGICAL PRESS

Collegeville, Minnesota

www.litpress.org

Cover design by Red+Company. Cover illustration by Philip Bannister.

1   2   3   4   5   6   7   8   9

Library of Congress Control Number: 2017935290

ISBN 978-0-8146-4663-2   978-0-8146-4687-8 (ebook)

Society proceeds sovereignly to eliminate the evil ones from her midst as if she were virtue itself. Like an honorable man killing his wayward son and remarking: "Really, I didn't know what to do with him." . . . To assert in any case, that a man must be absolutely cut off from society because he is absolutely evil amounts to saying that society is absolutely good, and no one in his right mind will believe this today.

—Albert Camus, *Reflections on the Guillotine*

Contents

Foreword

If the United States one day leaves the company of nations that still practice capital punishment, that may owe much to the efforts of one American nun, Sister Helen Prejean. Her classic work, *Dead Man Walking,* belongs in the company of such landmarks as Rachel Carson's *Silent Spring* and Harriet Beecher Stowe's *Uncle Tom's Cabin*: books that transformed consciousness and altered history.

The present biography tells the fascinating story that led up to Sr. Helen's book, and of her ongoing campaign, through tireless speaking and writing, to abolish the death penalty. Among the surprising stories is the account of her meetings with Pope John Paul II, and her influence in steering Catholic teaching toward an explicit rejection of capital punishment—a position explicitly embraced by Pope Francis and by the US Catholic bishops.

So identified is Sr. Helen with her cause that it is surprising to remember the substantial portion of her life spent in a more traditional form of religious life. From her Cajun roots in Baton Rouge, to her decision at the age of eighteen to enter the Sisters of St. Joseph, there was no foretelling her later role as one of the prophetic witnesses of our time. The most intriguing part of this story, in fact, is the gradual journey by which she came to understand the social implications of the Gospel.

In her early career, largely spent teaching in her order's schools, she had accepted the idea that the primary aim of Catholic life was to prepare believers for heaven—not to be concerned with worldly issues like poverty and injustice. But from the time she joined other sisters in moving into a housing project among poor African Americans, she began to read the Bible and to see the world around her through different eyes.

As Sr. Helen's story demonstrates, the Christian life entails a continuous call to conversion—a matter of responding to that voice that comes to us, through circumstances or the needs of our neighbors or our moment in history. It is a voice that calls us deeper into the heart of our vocation. In Sr. Helen's case, that voice came through a request to write to a prisoner on death row. That invitation, in turn, opened a door on a relationship that would change her life forever.

In the average life, such transformative opportunities may occur more often than we know. How often do we pass them by? Perhaps it may be in reading the story of this remarkable woman that we will confront the invitation to take our own first steps on the risky journey of faith.

—Robert Ellsberg

CHAPTER ONE

The Moment That Changed Her Life

Sister Helen Prejean is living on adrenaline and nerves. Last night sleep wouldn't come. At 3:00 a.m. she gives up. By 6:30 a.m. she's on her way from New Orleans to the Louisiana State Penitentiary in Angola and the "death house," the name for the part of the prison where inmates on death row are executed.

Waiting for her there is Elmo Patrick Sonnier—a thirty-four-year-old, white Cajun man scheduled to be executed by the electric chair in two days on April 5, 1984, at midnight. Sonnier and his brother Eddie abducted a teenage, white couple out for a night on lovers' lane in the fall of 1977. They raped the girl and then shot them both in the head after forcing them to lie face down on the ground. The state sentenced Pat to death by the electric chair. His brother Eddie received two life sentences.

Going through the prison on the way to see Pat, Sr. Helen passes out from hunger—she didn't eat that morning—and from a bronchial infection that's brewing in her lungs. She

1

ends up on a table in the prison hospital and learns this is where they will bring Pat after the execution to run an EKG. He may be the next person lying on that table, she thinks.

When prison officials return her to the death house, she learns no one told Pat what happened to her, and he worried that he would have to go through the execution alone. After a short prayer service with a priest chaplain where Pat receives Communion, Sr. Helen and he talk through a mesh screen and share stories to pass the time—some about their attempts with the governor for a stay of execution and some about small topics like birds and hunting. Sister Helen tries to wrap her mind around the fact that in a mere thirty hours or so, Pat could be dead. It's not like he has a terminal illness, just a scheduled execution. Pat admits he is afraid, but tells Sister they won't "break" him.

That night Sr. Helen stays at her mother's house, which is closer to Angola than her home in New Orleans. Family and friends join her. She takes a sleeping pill to help her rest. The next day, April 4, when she arrives at Angola it is a beautiful day—the sun is shining and the sky is blue. Sister Helen first stops to see Pat's brother Eddie Sonnier, who is also serving his sentences in Angola. News reports that morning feature stories about Eddie writing to the governor saying he committed the murders, not Pat, and that they planned to execute the wrong person.

Next Sr. Helen heads over to see Pat. At 3:15 p.m. a friend visits. No word yet from the governor or the courts on a stay of execution. Just after 5:00 p.m. the electrician arrives to make sure the chair is ready. At 6:00 p.m. it's time for Pat's final meal: a steak done medium well, potato salad, green beans, hot rolls with butter, a green salad, a Coke, and apple pie.

Soon they hear from the warden that the Fifth Circuit Court of Appeals turned down Pat's petition for a stay of execution. Now they wait for the governor. In the meantime, prison staff trickle in readying things for the execution. At 8:40 p.m. word comes from the attorneys that the governor also turned Pat down. As the guards shackle his hands and feet, Pat collapses to one knee, looks at her and says, "Sr. Helen, I'm going to die."

He makes out his will, leaving her all of his possessions and writes to his brother asking him to take care of himself and telling him that he loves him. Prison staff shave Pat's head and his eyebrows so they won't catch on fire during the execution. They also cut off his left pant leg and shave that leg.

At 11:30 p.m. the guards arrive to take Pat. They put a diaper on him, which angers him. Sister Helen is allowed to walk with Pat to the death chamber. He asks the warden if she can hold his arm. He agrees. It's the first time she's touched him. As they walk she recites the words of Isaiah 41:10, "Do not be afraid . . ."

The oak execution chair, nicknamed Gruesome Gertie, awaits Pat in the death chamber, which has the green walls and a clock ticking on the wall. Witnesses sit on the other side of the room behind glass. The fathers of the victims are there along with the press, Pat's attorneys, and the doctor who will verify his death. Sister Helen notices an exhaust fan running. It will remove the smell of burning flesh from the death chamber.

The warden asks Pat if he has any last words. He does. Pat asks for forgiveness from Lloyd LeBlanc, the father of David LeBlanc, one of the murdered teens. He says his brother committed the murders, but he is sorry all the same. No words for Godfrey Bourque, the father of Loretta Bourque. Pat knows Bourque has been speaking in the press about how much he has been looking forward to Pat's execution so he offers him no apology. Pat turns to Sr. Helen and tells her he loves her. "I love you too," she says.

Prison staff place a metal cap on Pat's head. It has an electrode attached to the top, which is connected to a wire that comes from a box behind the chair. Next they fasten an electrode to his leg, the one they shaved earlier. Then they strap his head to the chair with a piece of leather around his chin. Lastly they cover his face with a grayish-green cloth.

The warden nods to the executioner who flips a switch that pushes nineteen hundred volts of electricity through Pat, then five hundred, and then nineteen hundred again. A few minutes later the prison doctor pronounces Pat dead at 12:15 a.m., April 5, 1984.

On the way home from the prison, Sr. Helen's friends must stop the car so she can vomit. This early morning experience ends the two-year journey Sr. Helen made with Pat Sonnier. It also changes the course of her life and puts her on the road she calls a vocation from God as "death row's nun."

CHAPTER TWO

Her Early Years

Sister Helen Prejean is a diminutive woman and a force of nature. She's quick to laugh and quick to crack a joke. Her Southern drawl charms the audiences of this gifted storyteller—her voice lowers as she tells a serious or grim part of a story and rises at funny or exciting parts. She doesn't wear a habit; she keeps her hair short and dark, wears glasses, and has a cross around her neck and a simple, gold band on her left-hand ring finger.

Now in her seventies, Sr. Helen, a Sister of St. Joseph, continues to crisscross the country, speaking to anyone who will listen—church and school groups, university students, elected officials, and news media, to name a few. She speaks about the need to end capital punishment in the United States. It's a topic Sr. Helen knows a lot about since she has accompanied six people on death row to their executions and in recent years has taken up the cause for those unjustly condemned.

Even though she authored two books—one a national bestseller—and has an Oscar-winning movie about her ministry, along with a play and an opera, she doesn't rest on her laurels. Sister Helen continues to accompany people on death row, most recently Richard Glossip, who is on death row in Oklahoma. She has taken his case around the world and even to Pope Francis, petitioning for Glossip's exoneration because she believes he is innocent of the crime of which he was convicted.

She doesn't take time for pursuits like watching baseball or following the ins and outs of Hollywood. This woman has a mission from God, and it encompasses her entire being.

Helen was born on April 21, 1939, in Baton Rouge, Louisiana, to Louis and Gusta Mae Prejean (pronounced *pray-zhan*). She was the middle child between her sister Mary Ann and her brother Louie. The Prejean children had a privileged upbringing. Louis Prejean was a successful lawyer, and Gusta Mae was a nurse at Our Lady of the Lake Hospital in Baton Rouge. Theirs was a faith-filled, Catholic household.

The Prejeans prayed the rosary every night and on car trips. They attended devotions like Benediction at Sacred Heart Parish and instilled in Helen a love for the Mass. At one time, prior to their marriage, both Louis and Gusta Mae discerned calls to religious life. Her parents lived the faith they passed on to their children. Louis often helped people who couldn't afford legal representation and even helped some of them buy homes once they were back on their feet. Sister Helen recalls her mother, Gusta Mae, as a compassionate, warm, people person who would make little satin pillows for her patients who had abdominal surgeries so they could hold them when they coughed.

Louis and Gusta Mae laid the foundation for a strong prayer life that continues in Sr. Helen's life today. "What prayer is for me is listening. The basic prayer is 'What do you want me to do?' It's the invitation to come and just say,

'Is this what you want me to do?' Then to try to be able to do it in a spirit of calmness," she says.[1]

Despite her busy travel schedule, Sr. Helen finds time to pray while on the road. "I've learned how to do it in the air at thirty-five thousand feet. I'm on airplanes a lot so an airport can be my cloister," she says.[2] The anonymity of the airport also gives her time to read, to pray, and to be quiet in the Lord.

She feeds on the Scripture, often using the daily Mass readings as food for meditation. Sometimes something sparks, sometimes it doesn't, but she is faithful to setting aside time for contemplation, listening, and prayer so she's sure she's doing God's will in her life. "There is wholeness in it too—to be able to live a loving life and to be able to keep growing and stay on the edge," she says. "You don't say, 'Oh, well, I've done a few good things and I want to sit back. Hey, we've got a book; we've got a movie and an opera. We've won an Academy Award.'"[3]

It comes as no surprise Sr. Helen uses Mass readings for inspiration, since as soon as she could drive during her freshman year in high school, she started attending daily Mass. She went to the all-girls St. Joseph Academy in Baton Rouge, which was run by the Sisters of St. Joseph of Medaille (pronounced *may-die*).

Despite her religious upbringing, Sr. Helen was not a perfect, pious child. That title she gives to her elder sister Mary Ann whom she considers "wonderful," the better athlete, and the brave one.

"I was a crybaby. I was always being hurt," Sr. Helen recalls. "We would be with the boys, and they would have a swing. They would throw the rope up to you with the little wooden seat on it. You'd have to jump from the limb, grab the rope, and be on the swing. I was scared to death. I was the last one in the tree. I'm going, 'I don't want to fall.' Mary

Ann is going, 'Jump. Grab the rope.' "[4] It was the same on the diving board. Sister Helen, in her fear, would stand on the board afraid to jump. Everyone behind her yelled "Jump!" At the same time, Mary Ann did a perfect swan dive from the high board.

Growing up, the Prejean children often played on the family's five-acre property. Their mother regularly sent them outside to play. By the time they reached high school, the Prejean sisters were singing in the glee club. They always loved to sing. Helen sang soprano and Mary Ann sang second so they harmonized.

While the Prejeans sang often on family road trips, prayer never ceased to silence the kids. When the three kids were in the back seat of the station wagon getting punchy and rambunctious, Gusta Mae Prejean would say in a loud voice, "In the name of the Father, and the Son . . . " The next thing the kids knew they were praying the rosary and had calmed down. To this day, Sr. Helen calls it "Ritalin for kids." Those moments taught her how to pray and meditate.

The Prejean family laughed often and told stories. Helen was one of the extroverts. Mary Ann was the introvert. In high school, Helen took an interest in public speaking and entered oratorical contests. Mary Ann didn't like to speak out, but when her sister Helen ran for student body president, Mary Ann found her voice. "The whole school knew that Mary Ann was the one great in sports but didn't like to talk in public, so I asked her to be my campaign manager, and we blew the lid off the place," Sr. Helen recalls. Mary Ann stood up in front of the student body and said, "You all know I hate to give talks." Everybody in the audience is saying, "Yeah, yeah, yeah." She says, "But I'm here because I really believe my sister, Helen, will be the best student body president."[5] She won by a landslide.

The two sisters took different paths in their adult lives but remained close. Coming into adulthood in the 1950s left few options for women. If you didn't marry, you became a nun. Women who entered the "no-man's" space in between were pariahs. Helen never pictured herself marrying, having a family and a white picket fence. She wanted lots of time for her spiritual life. Early on, Helen desired to be a mystic like St. Teresa of Avila or St. Catherine of Sienna. A family didn't fit into that vision.

As Helen observed the culture, she saw that single women didn't have a real place but the nuns were alive, funny, and faith filled. The Sisters of St. Joseph at her high school were leading examples, taking students on retreats and teaching them how to pray better. In 1957 at age eighteen, Helen Prejean decided she was called to religious life and joined the community, taking the name Sr. Louis Augustine (after the Second Vatican Council she dropped the name for her own). She entered an apostolic community where they prayed like women in cloisters but also brought the Gospel out among the people through teaching.

The Sisters of St. Joseph trace their origins to Le Puy-en-Velay, France—a town in south central France located on the western side of the Loire River—where in 1650 Jesuit Fr. Jean Pierre Medaille drew together a group of women who desired to work for the poor and live lives steeped in faith. Le Puy is notable for other things besides the congregation's founding. The town's Cathedral of Notre Dame de Puy is one of the historic starting points for the St. James Way (El Camino), the famous pilgrimage route to Santiago de Compostela in Spain. More than 1,500,000 people walk a portion or all of El Camino each year. If that's not enough, a statue of Notre Dame de France stands high on a rocky outcropping, keeping watch over the town.

In the 1640s Fr. Medaille went to Le Puy as an itinerant missionary teacher, working in the towns in central and southern France and teaching youth in schools. Known as a gifted preacher and spiritual director, Medaille planted seeds of faith and inspired in others his vision of serving both the church and society as he went back and forth between the towns. In Le Puy he found a group of women eager to form a community around that purpose.

At that time, France was in turmoil. The country was involved in many battles and wars, both at home and abroad. As is often the case, the poor were most affected. The government increased taxes to pay for the military. Many people landed in debtors' prisons. Those battles left many widows and orphans in their wakes. Children were seen as a burden and often neglected or abused or both. Women turned to prostitution for income. The elderly and the sick who were poor languished. The situation was bleak.

France was a hierarchal society with rank and class determining wealth and economics. While France was a largely Catholic country, the church often neglected ministering to those living in the rural areas, who were largely poor and uneducated.

The hard times inspired some people to action. Six women came to Medaille and wanted to form a community that would help heal France through the Gospel. "Deep within they heard God's call to be instruments to bring about unity in a broken world—to do all in their power to heal; bridge ruptures; bring about harmony of persons with God and of persons with one another," wrote Sr. Eileen Mitchell in "Called to Inclusive Love: CSJ Charism, Spirituality, Mission."[6] John 17:21 inspired them: "As you, Father, are in me and I am in you, may they also believe in us, so that the world may believe that you sent me."

The spiritual and corporal works of mercy were their outline, which meant the women would not stay cloistered like the communities up until that point had done. They took their ministry to the people and served out in the community. This was new for the Catholic Church, and so naturally they faced some resistance from bishops.

Unlike today, the women religious at that time came only from wealthy families and brought their dowries into the community. Religious life called for solemn vows and prayer but also left time for intellectual and artistic pursuits. The famous St. Teresa of Avila was one of those women with a dowry who entered religious life, but thankfully was touched by God and went on to reform the Carmelite community. (In 1970 she was proclaimed the first female Doctor of the Church. A saint whose writings are beneficial to the entire church are proclaimed Doctors of the Church. The first doctors—Augustine, Ambrose, Jerome and Pope Gregory I—were declared in 1298.)

In the 1650s, women from the lower classes had no chance of entering religious life. However, prior to what Medaille called his "Little Design," some people had tried, including saints Angela de Merici, Francis de Sales, Jane de Chantal, Vincent de Paul, and Louise de Marillac. It was they who laid the groundwork for the Little Design to take root.

Instead of seeking papal approval for their endeavor, the first Sisters of St. Joseph set up informal houses, independent of each other, rather than a central house, to meet the needs of the local community. Unbeknownst to the founders, this set the stage for how the congregation would organize itself for hundreds of years. Instead of a traditional habit worn by nuns, the sisters donned the clothes of widows to avoid detection that might force them into cloisters. At that time the law considered widows free and competent, so this allowed the sisters to move easily among the people they served. Because the sisters lived among the poor and dressed like them, they visibly stayed within class divisions that didn't permit wealthy and noble-born people to mix with the poor.

Medaille and the founding women knew they needed support from the church to succeed long term, and they found it in the local shepherd Bishop Henri de Maupas of Le Puy. Maupas was a disciple of St. Francis de Sales and an advocate for the poor. On October 15, 1651, he offered his official ecclesiastical sponsorship of the new community and accepted their commitment as religious for his diocese.

Along with their spiritual formation, the congregation quickly identified the needs of the poor among them and devised ways to meet them. The charism drew women from around the country, and by the start of the French Revolution 150 years later, there were thirty communities around France with the support of the local bishops.

Soon after the French Revolution began in 1789, the government suppressed religious communities. It dissolved the Sisters of St. Joseph and confiscated their goods and possessions. The sisters were denounced as fanatics and enemies of the people and the revolution. Several sisters were imprisoned, and five died by guillotine.

Once the revolution ended, Catholic Church officials began to rebuild. A group of women came together in Lyon, France, as the "Black Daughters," seeking to pray and work with the poor. Cardinal Joseph Fesch of Lyon recognized the need to help the suffering of France and remembered the work of the Sisters of St. Joseph. He called upon Mother St. John Fontbonne who had joined the community in 1778 and survived the revolution. She answered.

On July 14, 1808, the women reconstituted a new congregation of the Sisters of St. Joseph. Through Mother

St. John, they had a direct connection to Medaille and the community's establishment in 1650, and they began to grow again and spread. In 1823 at the request of the bishop of Belley in southern France, Mother St. John sent a sister from her motherhouse to organize twenty-seven congregations serving in his diocese. They became the Sisters of St. Joseph of Bourg.

A rich French countess and a desperate bishop in Missouri were the means that brought the Sisters of St. Joseph to America in 1836. When Countess Felicite Rochejaquelein received word that Bishop Joseph Rosati in St. Louis needed help for his poor diocese, he told Mother St. John the countess would provide all the money they needed to answer his call. On March 5, 1836, six Sisters of St. Joseph arrived in New Orleans by boat and traveled up the Mississippi to St. Louis.

Since their early days in the United States, the Sisters of St. Joseph were independent diocesan congregations. Unlike other communities such as the Franciscans or Dominicans, each congregation was local to a certain region.

Sister Helen Prejean joined the Sisters of St. Joseph of Medaille, which had established its roots in Mississippi and Louisiana. Their first sisters arrived from France in 1854 from Bourg and ended up in Bay St. Louis, Mississippi, a town on the edge of the Gulf of Mexico and supported largely by fishing. They were sent there to start a school in nearby Waveland, located four miles away. Written histories of the community say that until the sisters could open a school in Bay St. Louis, they walked barefoot the four miles back and forth each day for several months so they could save their shoes.

As is the case for all pioneers, those early days were rough going. The sisters needed to adjust to the hot, humid weather and the Southern American version of English. However, they persevered and grew in numbers with both French women and native-born American women joining their ranks. They firmly put down roots in Louisiana, establishing convents in New Orleans, Baton Rouge, and New Roads, ministering as teachers and catechists to all people, no matter their race or class. Eventually members of the community branched out and established ministries "up north" in Ohio, Minnesota, Wisconsin, North Dakota, and Canada.

The sisters didn't take the name the Sisters of St. Joseph of Medaille until 1977 when the Vatican officially recognized this group of sisters, with roots in Bourg, France, as their own community. They chose the name after their founder, Jesuit Fr. Jean Pierre Medaille.

Some years before that, in the 1960s, congregations of the Sisters of St. Joseph in the United States who could trace their roots to Le Puy, France, united in a federation to preserve the unity of the spirit, charism, and history of the congregations. Later, in the 1990s, the federation divided itself into regions with the Sisters of St. Joseph of Medaille encompassing the communities in Cincinnati, Ohio; New Orleans, Louisiana; and Crookston, Minnesota. Today all of these communities dropped their town affiliations and are known as the Sisters of St. Joseph.

From her entrance into the Sisters of St. Joseph in 1957 until the early 1980s, Sr. Helen served as a teacher, novice master, and religious educator in a parish. She earned a bachelor's degree in English from St. Mary Dominican College in New Orleans in 1962. In 1973 she earned a master's in religious education from St. Paul University in Ottawa, Canada.

Reforms of the Second Vatican Council geared toward religious congregations of men and women energized Sr. Helen's community and moved them from a focus on education to a focus on social justice. In her book *Dead Man Walking*, Sr. Helen wrote of how she was a little reluctant to jump on the social justice bandwagon. Her understanding of faith and religious life was one of a personal relationship with God. Entering into social justice work wasn't easy or simple, and the answers to the problems weren't either.

It took Sr. Helen a long while before she grasped the social justice aspect of the Gospel. Part of it was because she was formed in a dualism straight out of the Greeks and Plato. She had learned that the eternal life, the unchanging eternal, is what lasts forever, and that the temporal, ephemeral, secular, transitive really doesn't last. With that formation, a person sought an eternal union with God.

Gradually she came to understand that it was a cohesive whole. Theology and the physical sciences existed and grew together. While it is imperative that every soul seeks heaven and the faithful are called to help others seek heaven, everyone is still called to help the poor, which Jesus said would always be among us. The church has long focused on justice for those on the margins. These teachings are commonly found in the social encyclicals such as *Rerum Novarum* (On the Condition of Labor) released by Pope Leo XIII in 1891; *Pacem in Terris* (Peace on Earth) released by Pope John XXIII in 1963; and *Evangelium Vitae* (The Gospel of Life) released by Pope John Paul II in 1995.

It didn't help that Sr. Helen didn't know any real poor people. "I was living in white privilege and living in an elite class—the educated. My daddy had money and I was separated from poor people. I wasn't mean or evil spirited, but I was simply naive and blind to the struggles of poor people," she says.[7]

Under her understanding, women religious were not social workers and were not meant to get involved in politics, become involved in social justice, or try to change things in the secular sphere. They were called to help everybody to know God. But Sr. Helen kept an open mind, and in 1980, at age forty, she "awakened to the Gospel of justice," she says. That awakening came as her community gathered to decide its ministries for the forthcoming decade. Sociologist Sr. Marie Augusta Neal of the Sisters of Notre Dame de Namur addressed the community during its gathering in Terre Haute, Indiana, and laid out the injustices going on in the United States and around the world. What were the Sisters of St. Joseph of Medaille going to do to relieve some of the poor's burdens, Neal challenged. The speaker proceeded to dismantle Sr. Helen's arguments that nuns weren't social workers and weren't political.

Neal talked about Jesus as the Good News for the poor. Of course God loved the poor, but it was not God's will for some people to be poor and some people to be rich. The theology Sr. Helen had studied never talked about resistance to the evils of poverty, or that poverty is not God's will. She accepted that some people were rich and some people were poor, and if poor people loved God and suffered with Jesus on the cross, one day they would have a higher place in heaven.

"That's about as naive as you can get when you're somebody who is privileged and never had to endure their suffering like lack of health care, your children or your husband dying, or you dying because you don't have health care," she says.[8]

Neal told the sisters that day that the Good News Jesus brings to the poor is that they would be poor no longer, that they had a right to resist poverty and work for what was rightfully theirs.

Sister Helen was raised in the Jim Crow days when whites and blacks were segregated. Jim Crow laws enforced segregation in Southern states on both a state and local level. The only African American people Helen met growing up were house servants. She knew their first names but not their last names. While her mom and dad were kind to the servants, they never questioned the system that subjugated black people as second-class citizens who couldn't even drink from the same water fountains as whites or sit with them in the movie theater. It was something the young Helen had not questioned. "Colored" and "White" signs hung over restroom doors, water fountains, and entrances designating who could use them. Segregation even existed in her home parish where black Catholics sat in a separate part of the church, and their children received the sacraments separately.

At age twelve, Helen witnessed her first physical attack against a black person. She and a friend were on the bus one day in December 1952 heading to do their Christmas shopping. She was in seventh grade. Life was good, and Helen and her friends were joking with each other during the ride.

When the bus reached their stop, and everyone was getting out, the driver shouted an obscenity to a young black woman and kicked her with his foot, throwing her off the bus. The woman fell to the sidewalk on her hands and knees, her purse flying open and coins spilling out onto the concrete. The young woman didn't say anything or look at the driver. She just picked herself up and walked away. Helen felt awful and the event stayed with her.

Memories like those continued to surface the longer Neal spoke during the seminar. The blinders fell from the nun's eyes, mind, and heart. Sister Helen entered the talk thinking, "I'm spiritual, I'm apolitical. I don't get involved in all the political stuff. We're nuns, we're not politicians." Neal blew through Helen's arguments. It was like she was reading

Sr. Helen's mind. Neal said, "You know, in a democracy, there's no apolitical stance to take. If you're not doing anything, then that means you're supporting the status quo and that is a very political stance to take." Sister Helen thought, "Dang, she got me—on Jesus and on the apolitical."[9]

Culture puts blinders on people and we say things like, "Well, honey, that's just the way we do things in the South. It's just better for the races to be separate," Sr. Helen says.[10] The privileged whites never questioned the rules because they had no experience of the suffering on the other side.

Something within her shifted during Neal's talk. Sister Helen likened it to the apostles at Pentecost. It was a real transformation that led her to act. She felt she couldn't do anything else.

After *Dead Man Walking* was released, Sr. Helen had the chance to thank Sr. Maria Augusta Neal for the talk she gave that converted her heart to the Gospel of social justice. Neal was "a steadfast prophet," Sr. Helen says, and woke her up to the needs of the poor.

Neal received a doctorate in sociology from Harvard in 1963 and chaired the sociology department at Emmanuel College, a Boston women's college run by her religious community. She was best known for conducting the National Sisters Survey, which charted change among US Catholic women religious after the Second Vatican Council. She published books on the state of religious life for women and conducted many studies on the state of the poor in the world, calling Catholics to close the gap between theology and poverty. She died in 2004 at the age of eighty-two.

"She taught the students all those years that the poor have a right to reach up for what is rightfully theirs. But on the other side of the equation are those of us who have been privileged who also have an obligation to be in solidarity with poor people and to share all of the suffering we've both been given," Sr. Helen says. "I hold her up as a true woman of the Gospel who stayed faithful and taught so many of us. Her work in sociology gave her first-hand knowledge of what was [happening] on the ground. I was never on the ground. I was always with privileged people. I was doing religious education and all that good stuff but I wasn't grounded in the suffering of people so I didn't feel compassion or passion to change things."[11]

Not long after Neal's talk to her community, in 1981 at age forty-one, Sr. Helen moved in with a few of her fellow sisters in the St. Thomas Housing Project, which at the time was the most dangerous housing project in New Orleans. They worked at Hope House, a social service agency in the projects that offered adult education classes, recreational programs, a food pantry, and homeless shelter.

Back in Baton Rouge, Sr. Helen's mother was "scared to death" for her daughter moving into "the Projects." For decades, the US government subsidized housing for the poor by building high-rise apartments in urban areas, which quickly became known as the Projects, a term originally ascribed to development projects. Constructed in clusters, these buildings quickly became areas of rampant violence and home to gangs, drug dealers, and addicts. The most notorious of the Projects was Cabrini-Green in Chicago, Illinois.

In one of her first days living in St. Thomas, bullets flew through the windows and tore apart one sister's dress hanging in the closet. Because of that, Sr. Helen's mother prayed daily at Mass for her daughter's safety. Women at St. Thomas More Parish, where her mother attended daily Mass, knew what ministry Sr. Helen was in by her mother's petitions during the Prayers of the Faithful. (This is a time during the

Mass when the community offers up specific prayer inten-
tions.) Gusta Mae Prejean regularly prayed for her daughter
working in the "ghetto."

While her family didn't visit often, once Sr. Helen's mother
summoned up the courage to visit her daughter for the
weekend. Her mother overcame her fear of the place because
she met the people. Those who don't live in these settings
hear news reports and assume the worst, but when they go
there and meet the people living there they see the humanity, Sr. Helen says. "There was violence there, but when you
meet the people it's just different. You're there and you're
in it with them."[12]

Living with the poor of St. Thomas opened Sr. Helen's
eyes to many injustices. It was like living in a war zone
where the language and the rules were different than what
she previously knew. She learned about government systems
and what happens to those in them. During those days half
of the adults in Louisiana did not graduate from high school,
one in every three babies was born to an unwed mother, and
the state had the nation's ninth highest crime rate.

The sisters were the only people who were not blacks in
those projects of fifteen hundred people. She met the working poor teaching those without high school diplomas at
Hope House. "I began to see from the underside what life
was like and how privileged I had been," she says. "I sat at
their feet and they became my teachers about everything.
The rules were different."[13]

Sister Helen worked with teen moms who had no chances
for college and who were the prey of any man who looked
at them. Rocking her baby in her arms, one young girl told
her she wanted to have a baby so she had something of her
own in the world. At St. Thomas, Sr. Helen saw how a boy
could make money running drugs down the block, but if he

took on a summer job his mother would lose the government support that kept them fed because his earnings would count against it. She noticed how murders of poor, black people didn't get reported in the news. At St. Thomas she learned how often poor, black people were incarcerated over people with money.

In *Dead Man Walking* she recalled helping single mother Shirley figure out how to make ends meet for her family on the food stamps and aid she received from the government. Shirley wanted to work, but if she took the job at the grocery store she would lose her health benefits and aid. Mothers like her who wanted to work faced additional expenses for childcare, medical treatment, and transportation. Her rent would also go up since in subsidized housing it is determined in proportion to a person's income.

The sisters at Hope House tutored preschoolers who didn't know words like "lettuce," "sofa," or "over." Without additional help as they entered the overcrowded city schools, they were bound to fail. Sister Helen saw for the first time how police treated the neighborhood residents. During the time she worked at Hope House, New Orleans received more complaints against the police than any other city in the country. Almost every family living in St. Thomas knew someone in prison.

Living with people doing the best they could in the circumstances of their lives made Sr. Helen appreciate the gifts of her own upbringing—a safe roof over her head, food on the table, an education, and the ability to read and write, to name a few. She also was forced into a simpler lifestyle. For example, no air-conditioning in the hot and humid Southern climate made her move slower and choose to do only essential tasks. She learned to appreciate gentle breezes and shade under trees. "And for the first time in my life I have the opportunity to enjoy the friendship of black people," she wrote in *Dead Man Walking*. "I realize how deprived my life was in the all-white-just-like-me social circles I used to frequent."[14]

It was also where God began her life's vocation with a single letter to a man on death row.

CHAPTER THREE

Patrick Sonnier

A simple, handwritten letter changed forever the lives of Sr. Helen Prejean and countless men and women on death row in the United States.

It was January of 1982. Chava Colon from the Prison Coalition in New Orleans asked Sr. Helen if she would consider becoming a pen pal to death-row inmate Elmo Patrick Sonnier, who was in the Louisiana State Penitentiary in Angola. She said yes.

Pat was a white, Cajun man from St. Martinville, Louisiana. He and his brother Eddie had been convicted of murdering two Catholic high school students on November 4, 1977. That night they abducted David LeBlanc, age seventeen, and Loretta Bourque, age eighteen, who were taking a night out on lovers' lane. They raped Loretta and forced her and David to lie down on the ground before shooting them both in the head.

Pat might not write back, Chava told her, but she figured that didn't matter because if he was on death row he was poor, and she was there to serve the poor. At the time, Sr. Helen was living and ministering in the St. Thomas Housing Projects in

New Orleans where she learned that "capital punishment means those without the capital get the punishment."[1] As a trained English teacher she also figured it was her duty to send some letters, maybe some poems.

That evening Sr. Helen sat down to pen her first letter, telling Pat about herself, the work she did, and that she would keep writing to him even if he didn't want to write back. She also included three photos—one of herself, one of Christ crucified, and one of a view of the water at Bay St. Louis, Mississippi. It was a step on a journey. "I never dreamed they were going to kill him or that I would be there. But, you see, we take a step," Sr. Helen says. "That's what it's like to follow grace, to follow a vocation. You take a step."[2] Along with his cell number, Pat's address at the prison included his location, death row—abbreviated D.R.

About a week later Pat replied to her letter. He wrote that he thought he could go it alone but couldn't and would be happy for a pen pal. At first he mistook the name "Helen" on the envelope for his former girlfriend and was going to tear up the letter. But he looked again and saw "Sister." A nun was writing him? Sisters had taught him in grade school, and he remembered some bad experiences with them, but Pat told Sr. Helen he still wanted her to write him.

He asked if they could just "talk regular" because he had a spiritual director in prison who talked a lot about Scripture, and Pat couldn't keep up. Sister Helen agreed and soon they were corresponding regularly. He wrote from his six-foot by eight-foot cell where he spent twenty-three of twenty-four hours of every day.

They shared stories. She often included news clippings or parts of the comics with her letters. He told her about life in prison and his cell. He even drew her a picture of his cell.

Sister Helen shared Pat's description of his cell in *Dead Man Walking*:

> On one wall is a bunk, on the back wall a stainless steel toilet and washbasin, a stainless steel plate above the wash-bowl instead of a mirror. He keeps all of his stuff in a footlocker under his bunk. He uses the footlocker for weight lifting. It's hard not to gain weight in this place, he says. Plenty of potatoes, rice, pancakes, and beans. He is allowed out of his cell for one hour a day (the time varies; the earliest is 5 a.m.) and then he can visit with the other eleven men on the tier if he chooses, but relations are often tense. If another inmate has it in for you, he explains, he can throw hot water on you through the bars of your cell, or he can take batteries out of his radio and sling them at you, or he can sling feces.[3]

In the beginning Pat frequently apologized for his pen-manship and asked Sr. Helen to tell him if she couldn't read his writing. It seemed such a trivial thing since the man was on death row. The letters were written in pen on yellow lined paper and were pristine with no corrections or imperfections. Later he revealed that he wrote several drafts of each letter to get them right. With time on his hands, if he made a mistake he just started over.

Soon Sr. Helen learned that inmates were given only two stamped envelopes a week to write letters, so she asked if she could send him stamps. That made him happy because then he could write her more often. The reality of prison life was always evident, because he told her to write inside the letter how many stamps she sent so he could make sure he got them. There was no telling who might take them when inspecting his mail since stamps were a commodity in prison.

They became steady pen pals, and Sr. Helen began to think of him as a fellow human being, not a criminal, but the reality of his crime was always there in her mind. It was a struggle for her to reconcile the easygoing Cajun who wrote to her with the brutal murderer of two helpless teenagers.

Pat regularly began his letters the same way: "I am hoping that when this letter reaches you that it will find you doing fine, and in the best of health. As for me I'm doing fine and in good health and I thank the good Lord above for that."

Contact from the outside world was important to those on death row. Many of their families were too poor to make regular visits to the prison, which was located in the center of Louisiana.

On many occasions, Pat included drawings on his letters and envelopes. He drew a few detailed schematics of the layout of his tier. Some of his drawings included the cartoon characters Tweety Bird and the Tasmanian Devil.

Sister Helen was getting an education about life on death row in Louisiana. Those on death row weren't allowed to work like other inmates, so they couldn't buy stamps or other items. One day Pat included a photo of himself taken in prison. "It is the first time I see his face: he's not scowling exactly but there is something about the bushy eyebrows and the way they slant downward. I feel a sliver of fear. I feel safer knowing he is behind bars," she wrote in *Dead Man Walking*.[4]

During their first few weeks of corresponding, Sr. Helen didn't look into the details of his case. Pat sounded like a regular person, but she couldn't help thinking of his crime, the victims, and the families left behind. She finally looked at the documents on file in Colon's office at the Prison Coalition that detailed the crime and the trials. After one look,

Sr. Helen realized there was some knowledge that would change you forever.

There was gruesome testimony detailing the manner of Loretta Ann Bourque and David LeBlanc's deaths and how two men fitting Pat and Eddie Sonnier's descriptions had been terrorizing couples at lovers' lane during the weeks leading up to the murders. Sister Helen felt rage over the crimes and at the same time guilt for befriending the brothers. But she felt in her heart that everyone has a right to life no matter the worst thing he or she did. All the while she also knew she was in over her head.

Then Sr. Helen read about contradictions in the brothers' confessions. At first, Pat confessed to shooting the teens, but at his trial he said his brother did it. At Pat's trial, Eddie told the jury that his brother pulled the trigger. Both men admitted to the kidnappings. Pat denied raping Loretta, but Eddie said they both did.

In separate trials both brothers were convicted of first-degree murder and sentenced to death. The Louisiana Supreme Court later overturned both convictions—for Eddie it was because they felt Pat was the shooter and more culpable; for Pat it was because of a judge's error. However, at Pat's second sentencing trial he was once again given death despite Eddie testifying that he himself shot the teens, saying that he snapped at that moment and was afraid to admit the murders earlier. The court said Eddie was just trying to spare his brother from the electric chair.

Reading these documents left Sr. Helen shaken. She wrestled with the guilt of befriending the teens' murderer but at the same time had a growing unease about the morality of the death penalty. What would she feel if one of her family members was murdered—rage, loss, helplessness? At the same time Sr. Helen was convinced that Jesus wouldn't want us to kill another human being, no matter the circumstances. She was also convinced that if she herself were murdered, she wouldn't want her murderer executed, "especially by government—which can't be trusted to control its own bureaucrats or collect taxes equitably, or fill a pothole, much less decide which of its citizens to kill."[5] This argument of imperfect governments and legal processes would become a common refrain in Sr. Helen's work against capital punishment.

In the meantime, the letters from Pat continued. She noticed how he always thanked her at the end for writing to him and caring about him. He was lonely. Did anyone ever visit him? No, he wrote. So Sr. Helen arranged to visit, but before that could happen Pat had to put her name on his official visitor list. There were two categories on that list: visitor or spiritual director. He chose spiritual director. It was a pivotal choice on both Pat's and Sr. Helen's journeys because spiritual directors could be with the inmate right up to one's execution and could witness the execution. It was the time leading up to and including his death that Sr. Helen later felt God was calling her to witness. Executions occurred in the early hours of the morning with little transparency to the conditions. It was a secret ritual that later on she felt she must share with the world.

Several months after Pat put her on his visitor list, Sr. Helen had an interview at the prison and was then cleared to be Pat's spiritual director. Their first meeting would be on September 15, 1982. That day she drove the three hours from New Orleans to Angola and went through the prison's processing. Guards yelled, "Woman on the tier," and led her to a green metal door with a barred window and the words "death row" written across the top in red block letters. She was ushered behind four locked doors into a room with six visiting booths. Heavy mesh screens divided the visitors from the inmates.

Then Pat walked in wearing a blue denim shirt and jeans. His hands were cuffed to a brown leather belt around his waist. "Boy, am I glad to see you, Sister," he told her. They had two hours to talk. Pat was open and friendly, telling her about all of the letters he had received from pen pals Sr. Helen had set him up with. "I was always a loner growing up. I've never had so many friends,"[6] he said. Pat told her he kept a checklist in his cell of "letters received" and "letters answered" with dates next to each.

During their first meeting, he chain smoked, leaning down to light his cigarette in his cuffed hands. The whole experience was surreal to Sr. Helen: traveling to meet a man condemned to death, meeting a man who had killed two people, looking at his hands as he talked, and thinking about those hands pulling a trigger. On that day Pat had a gift for her. He made her a picture frame out of folded cigarette wrappers. This was Pat's second time in Angola prison. Previously he had served time there for stealing a truck.

Going into the visit, Sr. Helen worried how they would fill the two hours, but Pat kept talking the whole time, telling stories about growing up and about his daughter who lived with foster parents in Texas. Two hours passed quickly, and Sr. Helen said good-bye to Pat. Her first visit to death row was over. On her way home she realized how tense she was the entire time, and she craved a shower to wash away the feel of the prison. She also knew she would return because Pat had never felt a steady love from anyone in his life. She could give him that.

Just how much her visits meant to him comes out in his letters. "You know after our visit I felt so good that I came back to my cell and I wrote seven letters and I didn't mess up one of them. For I usually have to start them over at least three times before I get them right," Pat wrote on December 2, 1982.[7]

All the while, lawyers were petitioning on Pat's behalf for a stay of execution. They hoped to have his sentence overturned to life in prison, like his brother Eddie. The stress of it all came out in his letters.

In some of his letters, Pat wrote that his "nerves" bothered him. In one instance it was because a fellow inmate on death row was taken for execution but received a stay at the last minute. When someone is taken away to Camp F—the area of the prison that houses the electric chair—it affects many of the inmates, especially if they are friends.

"For I'm doing much better now that Tim got his stay, for I must say that it did have me feeling down and out. . . . Tim and I still talk through the bars for he's still not quite himself yet, for he tries to say that it doesn't bother him. But I happen to know better than that. Because it still bothers me and I know that it has to bother him," Pat wrote.[8]

Pat's first execution date was August 19, 1983. When Sr. Helen visited him the day before, Pat finally talked about the murders. He had lost thirty pounds in two weeks because the anxiety and stress made it impossible for him to eat. He lived on coffee and cigarettes. Later Sr. Helen learned it was common for the condemned to lose extreme amounts of weight leading up to their execution.

The warden gave her four hours to visit with Pat the day before that first execution date. During that time both she and Pat anxiously waited to hear from the attorneys about a possible stay of execution. "I want to be with you when you die," she told Pat. He said no because he thought the experience would scar her. "I can't bear the thought that you would die without seeing one loving face. I will be the face of Christ for you. Just look at me," Sr. Helen told him.[9] She had come to love him as a brother and wanted to be there for him. He agreed. He wondered about the execution. Would he feel pain? Would he feel the burning? He worried about his mother.

Sister Helen asked Pat if he believed God had forgiven him for the murders. Yes, he said, adding that he had gone to confession earlier to the elderly priest-chaplain. He said that every night before bed he knelt down and prayed for the teens and their families, and said he would go to his grave feeling bad about their murders. Despite his words, Sr. Helen tried to determine if he was sincere. Did Pat really feel remorse for the part he played in the deaths of David LeBlanc and Loretta Bourque?

Nobody was supposed to die that night, Pat told Sr. Helen that afternoon in August 1983. His brother Eddie snapped. Eddie had recently been released from jail for harassing a girl who was pregnant with his child but who wouldn't marry him. He had gone over to her house with a sawed-off shotgun and threatened to kill her and her entire family. Eddie also cut the phone wires. He was arrested and thrown in jail.

When he came out of jail he wasn't the same. "Something I think the boy David said to him teed him off and he shot the kids," Pat told Sr. Helen. "I should've known he could blow. I should not have let us get mixed up in the bad things we was doing."[10] While fleeing from the police in the days after the murders, the brothers planned to both confess to the killings because they thought the police wouldn't know who actually pulled the trigger. Eddie didn't follow the plan.

As she left the prison that August day, trying to determine if Pat meant what he said, she heard on her car radio that he was granted a stay while the Fifth Circuit Court of Appeals heard his petition. Two months later, in October, the court denied his petition. Time was running out so Sr. Helen contacted Millard Farmer, an attorney she had heard of who defended death-row prisoners. Between Farmer and Sr. Helen, they pulled out all the stops, working the courts, the governor, and church leaders. Sister Helen asked the state's Catholic bishops to write to Louisiana's then-governor Edwin Edwards. On February 21, 1983, the US Supreme Court denied Pat's appeal. His new execution date was set for April 5, 1984.

Pat's anxiety over his future surfaced again in his letters to Sr. Helen. He was "not doing so great with my nerves" because a court had denied his appeal. "For I heard it on TV yesterday and even though I already knew that they were going to turn me down it still kind of got to me. I don't know why it got to me for it had never did before," he wrote. It's important in prison not to show emotion so he says he tries to keep himself together "for I don't want to let it show that it's getting to me because these people here enjoy seeing that it bothers you."[11]

He also wrote that he was worried about how his daughter Star, his mother, and his brother Eddie were taking the news. Just like anyone else, inmates have families, and many worry about them. In Pat's case, he worried most about his daughter. "Well the thing that I find the hardest is not being able to be there watching Star growing up and how Star will take it if I should be executed for that's the hardest thing for me Sr. Helen!"[12]

In the meantime, the lawyers arranged a hearing with the state's five-member pardon board, appointed by the governor. But clemency was denied again. At the request of Sr. Helen, her fellow Sisters of St. Joseph began making arrangements for Pat's funeral, including finding a suit for his body. The sisters agreed that Pat could be buried among the sisters in their plots, and they found a funeral home willing to donate its services.

The correspondence between Sr. Helen and Pat ended with his final letter to her dated April 1, 1984—just days before he was put to death in the electric chair. He thanked her for everything she did for him, which included working with lawyers to get him off death row and visiting his family back home.

"I just thank God above for sending you into my life, for since I've met you my life had meaning. And I was so very blessed when you came into my life, and want to tell you that I love you and that our friendship meant so very much to me Sr. Helen!"[13]

He asked her to look after his family and told her she was the most important person in his life, but not in a romantic way, he clarified as he had done on other occasions. He didn't want to give the wrong impression. "Because I know that I mean a lot to you because you have done everything in your power to save my life and I know this is true because I've seen it and I've felt it deep down in my heart and soul, Sr. Helen!"[14] He closed by wishing her a happy birthday. Her birthday was April 21.

Two days before Pat's scheduled execution, Sr. Helen visited the prison, stopping by to see Eddie first. During the time she was writing to and visiting Pat, Sr. Helen struck up a correspondence with his brother Eddie. Eventually Sr. Helen also became Eddie's spiritual advisor and began visiting him.

Eddie handed her a letter addressed to the governor saying they were killing the wrong brother. Prisoners weren't allowed to bring letters to the visiting room so Sr. Helen showed it to the guard. Eventually the prison warden gave permission for Sr. Helen to take the letter. The guards told her that word in the prison was that they were executing the wrong brother.

In his first few letters, also handwritten in pen on lined paper, Eddie addressed the letters "Sr. Prejean," but called her "Mrs. Prejean" throughout, as if he were not exactly sure she was a nun.[15] When filling out the form to request her as his spiritual advisor, he wrote that the form asked if she were married, and he wasn't sure of that answer.

Since Eddie was not on death row, he was allowed to earn money working in nearby cotton fields, and twice a week he "bled" to earn money to send to his brother, Pat, who was not allowed to work. Sister Helen arranged for money to be sent to Pat so Eddie didn't have to sell his blood anymore.

"To ask people to share with my brother so that I wouldn't have to sell my blood, it brings tears to my eyes for no one in my family but my mother even cared if I was getting sick because I was selling my blood," Eddie wrote on February 7, 1983.[16]

Even though he wouldn't be killed like his brother, the burden of a life sentence without parole weighed on Eddie, especially when his mother asked during a visit when he would be coming home. "I tell you what Sr. Helen I wish they would have went ahead and killed me instead of taking the death sentence away and giving me life. For it's killing me slowly every day, Sr. Helen," Eddie wrote on April 24, 1983.[17]

While in prison together the brothers had been writing one another, but prison officials weren't delivering the brothers' letters. Eddie sent a letter to Pat through Sr. Helen where he again admitted to killing the young couple.

"I sure hope he [Pat's lawyer] can find something that will make them people understand that you didn't do the killings, that I did. You know bro, you should never said that you did the killings just to try and get me off. Because now they don't want to believe that you didn't do it."[18]

Next, Sr. Helen visited Pat. They were both tense. Guards watched his every move and would continue to do so until his execution. They didn't want him killing himself before his execution. "They're not going to break me," he told Sr. Helen. "I just pray God give me strength to make that last walk."[19]

The day after Pat was executed, his funeral Mass took place at a funeral home in Baton Rouge, the same one where Sr. Helen's uncle had been laid out years earlier. It was where she had first seen a dead body. Roselawn Cemetery, also in Baton Rouge, was Pat's final resting place, right alongside deceased Sisters of St. Joseph. While his mother didn't attend the funeral—she felt it would be too difficult for her—Pat's daughter Star was there, and the prison let his brother Eddie come, complete with the requisite shackles around his hands and feet. Bishop Stanley Ott, the then-bishop of Baton Rouge officiated.

Reporters at the cemetery questioned Sr. Helen about her feelings for Pat. Was she in love with him, they asked. "No, I tell them, I loved Pat as a sister loves a brother, as Jesus taught us to love each other; it was not a romantic relationship."[20]

The call from God to dedicate her life to ending the use of the death penalty came to Sr. Helen after leaving what she calls the prison's "death chamber" at Angola.

"When I came out, I had watched a man be zapped, killed in an electric chair, and it was in the middle of the night," Sr. Helen recalls. "And then I realized, it was so clear and it stuck. That's how I knew it was grace. I can have great ideas, but if they don't stick then they'll never be a commitment.

These were the words of it: 'People are never going to be close to this. This is a secret ritual done in the middle of the night. They're going to read the papers the next day and say justice was done. Look at the terrible crime. Pat and his brother had killed two innocent teenagers in cold blood. It was outrageous.' "[21]

God brought Sr. Helen in as a witness to what happens when the state executes its people. And God called her to take people on this journey so they can also make it in their hearts. Most people, at one time or another, when they hear of a horrible crime, feel that the perpetrator deserves to die. "They don't see it. It's easy to kill somebody when you think of him or her as a monster, an animal," she says. "But it's really hard to kill a human being and that's part of the story that's in *Dead Man Walking*."[22]

CHAPTER FOUR

Dead Man Walking

Sister Helen left the death chamber on April 5, 1984, knowing God was telling her to be a witness to the secret ritual of legal execution and to share her experience with the world.

When you are raised in the South, talking is what you do, and storytelling comes naturally, especially to Sr. Helen. So she went on the road, telling the story of Patrick Sonnier's execution to anyone who would listen—church groups, social justice sympathizers, university crowds. She thought, "Let me get on the road, talk about this, and bring people through the experience."[1] And she told stories to bring listeners over both arms of the cross.

While initially some of the sisters in her community questioned her association with "murderers," the entire congregation supported and stood behind her new ministry.

In 1990 the community took a public stance against the death penalty and adopted a statement that read in part, "We cannot uphold a practice which permanently banishes some of our members from the human family by killing them. . . . As followers of Jesus Christ we reaffirm his way of compassion, which calls us to overcome hatred with love, to meet evil with goodness, and to forgive rather than avenge ourselves on those who harm us."[2]

A short time later people started to say to Sr. Helen, "You should write a book about this." At the time she didn't understand what power a book could have to advance the message of the injustice of the death penalty. To her, writing a book meant withdrawing to a cave for two years scribbling away in solitude. Then, who would read the book?

But she began to write. The first thing she wrote was an essay for *St. Anthony Messenger* magazine about going to pray with the father of David LeBlanc, who was murdered by Patrick Sonnier. She and Lloyd LeBlanc prayed the rosary at a little Catholic church during an hour of Eucharistic adoration. It was a compelling Catholic story because it involved praying the popular Marian prayer of the rosary, and she was the spiritual director to the man who killed LeBlanc's son.

After that first essay, she continued to write. Slowly the structure of the book began to form in her mind, but Sr. Helen wasn't sure God wanted her to write a book in the first place. One of her religious community's mottos is "Don't get out ahead of grace," and she wasn't about to do that. She wanted a clear sign from God. After all, books on the death penalty already existed. Why would hers be needed?

She decided to send some of her writing to her friend Bill McKibben, who had published several books on environmental issues. He liked what he read and gave her the name of his literary agent in New York City. That was Gloria Loomis; the agency she worked for had been around since the 1940s and specialized in books of social importance.

Next thing Sr. Helen knew, she had an agent. She sent Loomis a proposal and a couple of chapters for what would become *Dead Man Walking: An Eyewitness Account of the*

Death Penalty in the United States. (Prison guards used to call out the phrase "Dead man walking" as they led a prisoner to the death chamber.)

Loomis loved it and walked the proposal down the street to Random House and Jason Epstein, the publishing house's editorial director at the time. After reading the proposal and sample chapters, Epstein invited Sr. Helen to New York City to discuss the book. "It was the most intelligent conversation I had with anybody about the death penalty," Sr. Helen recalled. "And he said, 'We'll give you a contract.' "[3]

The nun from Louisiana left the offices of Random House with a contract under her arm to write a book and an advance of about $20,000 that would go to her community. That was 1991. She said to herself that day, "Well, God, this must be what you want me to do."

The reality of the whole whirlwind experience—that a never-before published Catholic nun now had a contract with a big-time publisher to tell a story about the death penalty—took some time to sink in, but she had great aspirations for the book. She told the *New York Times Magazine*: "I want the book to be a bridge between the poor and nonpoor. . . . I am hoping that when people of good will read it, they won't allow the death penalty to continue."[4]

Two years later she finished the book; Epstein was with her along the way as a hands-on editor. After she wrote the first draft, the two sat down and talked it over. He used his expertise to shape the book.

Some of the best advice Epstein gave Sr. Helen was to talk about Patrick and Eddie Sonnier's crime early on in the book and not bury it. "You wait far too long in this story before you talk about the crime and how horrified you were that these two teenagers were killed," he told her. If she didn't introduce it sooner, readers would easily dismiss her story and say, "Oh, she's a Catholic nun. She believes in Jesus so this was easy for her." They would think she couldn't really face the crime head on and would expect every spiritual platitude from her. "If you don't stand in the horror of that crime in the first ten pages, then no one is going to read your book," Epstein told Sr. Helen.[5]

Random House released *Dead Man Walking* in 1993, but Sr. Helen, then age fifty-three, still had doubts about its success. What were the chances of success for a book by a Catholic nun on the death penalty, which at the time was at its peak in the number of executions in the United States?

However, the book had the editorial director of Random House personally pulling for it. After the new books for that year were announced, Epstein stood before the publishing house's sales representatives and held up *Dead Man Walking*. He said, "See this book? This book is going to do what Rachel Carson did with *Silent Spring*. It's going to change the discourse on the death penalty."[6]

The next thing Sr. Helen knew she was doing lots of interviews with the news media and big promotional events. The book received rave reviews.

The *New York Times* said of the book, "Sr. Prejean, a member of the Sisters of St. Joseph of Medaille, is an excellent writer, direct and honest and unsentimental; her accounts of crime and punishment are gripping, and her argument is persuasive. But it is her personality that makes this book so powerful. Quoting Gandhi and Camus, reflecting on her childhood in Baton Rouge in the 1940s and 50s, grappling with her responsibility to the families of murder victims, she almost palpably extends a hand to her readers. Here I am, she seems to be saying; where are you on this issue?"[7]

She made an appearance on the *Today Show,* and the *New York Times Magazine* did a profile on her. This was noteworthy because she was an unknown, first-time author. The interview was published May 9, 1993, and written by Sue Helpren. "Its power comes as much from the relentless pace of her narrative as it does from the undistorted portraits she draws of the men whose deaths have been scheduled by the state," Helpren wrote. "She doesn't suppose their innocence, doesn't appeal to the possibility that somehow they are there by mistake. She embraces their guilt, and from that embrace argues that 'people are more than the worst thing they have ever done in their life.' "[8]

That quote—"people are more than the worst thing they have ever done in their life"—became the most popular one attributed to Sr. Helen, and she has repeated those words countless times since.

In Sr. Helen, Random House recognized an author who would be on a permanent book tour. For as long as she was able, Sr. Helen would be on the road taking people through the experience of the death penalty and promoting *Dead Man Walking.* That has been the case ever since.

In 2006 Random House published her sequel to *Dead Man Walking,* titled *The Death of Innocents: An Eyewitness Account of Wrongful Executions*, which profiled two men unjustly accused and convicted of crimes and sentenced to death. The publisher was committed to ending the death penalty in the United States like she was and told her that in *Dead Man Walking* they began the discourse with the American public for ending the death penalty. In *The Death of Innocents* they would finish that discourse and bring it to an end.

Dead Man Walking sat at number one on the *New York Times* best-seller list for thirty-one weeks and earned a

Pulitzer Prize nomination. An international hit, the book was also translated into ten languages. In 2013 Random House Penguin Group released a twentieth anniversary edition with a foreword by humanitarian Archbishop Desmond Tutu and afterwords by Susan Sarandon and Tim Robbins.

At the time of the book's original release, Sr. Helen didn't know actress Susan Sarandon or actor/director Tim Robbins, but they would play a major role in her future.

After the book achieved such success, Sr. Helen's congregation, the Sisters of St. Joseph of Medaille, signed a film option with a producer. However, a film never panned out. Leery of how nuns had been portrayed in movies in the past, the congregation and Sr. Helen wanted a realistic portrayal of the events and were careful with whom they wanted to make a film version. Sister Helen was advised that if she gave her story to someone to make into a film, she must be able to trust them because they could change the whole thing if they chose to.

Then movie star Susan Sarandon read *Dead Man Walking* and reached out to Sr. Helen. The Hollywood actress believed the book would make a great movie, and she wanted to play the part of Sr. Helen. In interviews, Sarandon has said she was a little wary of meeting a nun because she didn't have fond memories of them from her days in Catholic school. The actress immediately inspired trust in Sr. Helen.

Sarandon said her then-partner Tim Robbins should direct the film, and Sr. Helen said okay. Sarandon gave a copy of the book to Robbins, who starred in such films as *The Shawshank Redemption* and *The Player*. She wanted them to make it into a movie together. Robbins took his time reading it, however, since he was working on *The Player*. It all came down to what he called an "altercation on Sixth Avenue in New York" where Sarandon asked him if he was going to read the book. If not, she would find someone else to help her make the film. Susan Sarandon told news media that she wanted to portray Sr. Helen because she wasn't a hero. She was just a regular person in over her head.

Finally Robbins read the book and agreed with Sarandon. He wrote the screenplay and directed and produced the movie. Like Sarandon, Robbins was raised Catholic and attended Catholic schools. Robbins contacted actor Sean Penn to play the lead character of Matthew Poncelet. The congregation received $150,000 for the rights for the film, and Sr. Helen had approval of the script. Robbins secured $12 million in funding, which was a low-budget film at the time.

At one point the financiers reduced funding and assumed everyone would work for less pay. Robbins and Sarandon agreed to work at a lower rate, but they weren't sure what Penn would say. When approached, Penn agreed, quickly saying it didn't matter. He really wanted to play the part of Poncelet. Penn told Sr. Helen that he cried after reading the script of *Dead Man Walking*. When that happens, you have to do the part, he told her.

They went through five drafts of the script. Robbins quipped in a 2014 appearance at DePaul University in Chicago that it was the first time since grade school that a nun had corrected his grammar.

In *Dead Man Walking*, Sr. Helen wrote about accompanying two men to their deaths, but one of the first big changes Robbins made to the story was to amalgamate them into the character of Matthew Poncelet. He also changed the characters' names because the murders were still fresh in the minds of the people involved. In her book, it's questionable if one of the men, Pat Sonnier, actually shot the victims, which was the crime he was executed for. The other man, Robert Lee Willie, was clearly guilty. Since people can easily agree that an innocent person should not be killed, Robbins wanted the character to be guilty and unlikeable. That would force viewers to wrestle with the question of whether or not it is right to kill even the most despicable person.

While Robbins changed the names of the other characters, he kept Sr. Helen as herself. He shared that news with her on an escalator in LaGuardia Airport in New York City. That's when she realized her name would be out there for the world. Sister Helen's notoriety increased once the movie was released, as did sales of her book.

Sister Helen didn't always agree with Robbins's proposed changes along the way. In the book, Sr. Helen recounted a scene where she met with a priest-chaplain affiliated with the Louisiana State Penitentiary in order to be cleared to visit Pat Sonnier as his spiritual director. The priest suggested she wear her habit when she visited death row. That was a suggestion she ignored. When writing the script, Robbins had Sr. Helen going back to her car and pulling out a habit. "I told Tim, 'No way!' We don't wear habits, and I had to explain to him the reasons for that," said Sr. Helen in an interview with *St. Anthony Messenger* magazine. "I teased him. I said, 'Boy, you better get the nuns right in this! We haven't had a good film about nuns since The Bells of St. Mary's.'"[9]

In reality, both men whom Sr. Helen wrote about in *Dead Man Walking* were killed by electrocution. In addition to combining those two men into the one character of Matthew Poncelet, Robbins also changed the method of execution to lethal injection. While the scene of death by electric chair would be great filmmaking, Robbins told Sr. Helen he didn't want to give viewers any "moral outs" when watching the film. At that time states were abandoning the electric chair for the more "humane" way of killing by lethal injection. He felt it would be easy for viewers to oppose electrocution but accept lethal injection, and he wanted to challenge them. Sr. Helen agreed.

After receiving the final funding and the go-ahead to make the film, Robbins called Sr. Helen to tell her the good news. He said he was scared, Sr. Helen says, and that reassured her they picked the right director. They filmed in New York and on location in Louisiana over nine weeks.

As a script consultant, Sr. Helen was on the set for the filming and on more than one occasion she would be transported back to the real moment that the actors were portraying. The first scene they filmed was Sr. Helen meeting with a victim's family. They chose a setting in Slidell, Louisiana, a suburb of New Orleans. Robbins gave her a set of headphones so she could listen to the dialogue. While watching Sarandon, she was taken back to the real moment. She felt it all—the family's loss, her own grief and despair, everyone's pain. It was like a cauldron of emotions. Sarandon was a window that took Sr. Helen right back to what had happened.

One scene that people often tell her stays with them happens leading up to Poncelet's execution. The character's mother and brothers visit him in prison. No one knows what to say to each other so the room is silent except for the squeaking coming from the youngest brother's shoes as he moves back and forth across the room. The awkwardness of visiting a loved one whom you know will be killed in a few hours leaves many of the families without words and the room silent, says Sr. Helen, who also made a cameo in the film. She was part of the vigil outside of the prison on the eve of Poncelet's execution—the woman holding the candle.

The sets accurately recreated the death row cells and other areas in the Angola prison. The killing devices—including the crucifix-like table from which an elevated Sean Penn says his final words—were exact replicas of execution gear from Louisiana and Missouri.

The most poignant moment of filming for Sr. Helen came during the scene where Penn's character was blaming everyone for his plight, and Sarandon challenged him to face the truth of what he had done. The intensely emotional scene took seven takes, and each time Sr. Helen cried. "I guess in a way it was also this great release for me to see it, to be back from it. Because it was the moment of redemption and transformation. Afterwards I just went and I hugged Tim," she said in an interview.[10]

Along the way, Sr. Helen, Robbins, and Sarandon became friends. She often stayed with them when in New York and even took a trip with them and their children to Washington, DC.

Dead Man Walking was released to limited US audiences in December 1995 and received rave reviews. Its wide release to cinemas across the country was two months later, in February 1996. Popular theater critic Roger Ebert gave it four stars, the highest rating he gave to movies.

"Sr. Helen, as played here by Sarandon and written and directed by Tim Robbins (from the memoir by the real Helen Prejean), is one of the few truly spiritual characters I have seen in the movies," Ebert wrote. "Movies about 'religion' are often only that—movies about secular organizations that deal in spirituality. It is so rare to find a movie character who truly does try to live according to the teachings of Jesus (or anyone else, for that matter) that it's a little disorienting: This character will behave according to what she thinks is right, not according to the needs of a plot, the requirements of a formula, or the pieties of those for whom religion, good grooming, polite manners and prosperity are all more or less the same thing."

Ebert was moved by how the movie was spiritual without being conventional or pandering. Sister Helen didn't try to convert Poncelet, didn't fall in love with him, and didn't try to claim he was innocent and work for his release.

"This is the kind of movie that spoils us for other films, because it reveals so starkly how most movies fall into conventional routine, and lull us with the reassurance that they will not look too hard, or probe too deeply, or make us think beyond the boundaries of what is comfortable," Ebert wrote. "For years, critics have asked for more films that deal with the spiritual side of life. I doubt if 'Dead Man Walking' was what they were thinking of, but this is exactly how such a movie looks, and feels."[11]

Moviegoers were equally moved. Theater managers told Tim Robbins that they had never known a film when at the end of it everybody stayed glued to their seats until the screen went black. They reported that audiences then filed out in silence.

It was nominated for Oscars in four categories: best leading actor (Penn), best leading actress (Sarandon), best directing (Robbins), and best original song ("Dead Man Walking," written and performed by Bruce Springsteen). Sarandon took home the Oscar for best actress.

Sister Helen was in the audience when Sarandon won her Oscar. During her acceptance speech, Sarandon thanked members of the Academy for choosing her and thanked them for giving her the opportunity to thank "the people who are so dear to my heart."

"First of all, Sr. Helen Prejean who is here tonight," she said, gesturing to the area of the auditorium where Sr. Helen was sitting, "for trusting us with your life and bringing your light and your love into all of our lives." Wrapping up her four-minute speech, the actress said, "May all of us find in our hearts and in our homes, and in our world, a way to nonviolently end violence and heal."[12]

Sister Helen was convinced that the film would ultimately take the story of the injustice of the death penalty to ever more people. More than 1.3 billion people watched the Academy Awards that night, which was the feast of the Annunciation. "It's a brave, good film that brings people fairly over to both sides and lets the audience figure it out for themselves," Sr. Helen says.

In 1998 Sr. Helen asked Robbins to write a play adaptation. She had read a *New Yorker* article that said Arthur Miller's *Death of a Salesman* had been performed more than one million times. If there were a play version of her book, even more people would be informed about the injustices of the death penalty.

Robbins didn't want to do something on Broadway so they looked at writing something that could be performed at colleges, universities, and high schools. As a requirement to obtain the rights to the play, the schools would have to convince two other departments to offer classes on the death penalty at the same time. Both Robbins and Sr. Helen wanted to encourage conversation about the issue among younger Americans. Since the Dead Man Walking School Theatre Project launched in 2004, more than two hundred schools around the country performed the play. The project held its final season in 2015.

In 2000 *Dead Man Walking* came to the stage again, this time as an opera. Lotfi Mansouri, then-general director of the San Francisco Opera, wanted a new opera for his company and commissioned Jake Heggie to write the music. It was a risky move on Mansouri's part because while Heggie was a successful songwriter, he had never written an opera. Mansouri asked playwright Terrence McNally to work with Heggie, and it was McNally who came up with the idea to make an opera out of *Dead Man Walking*. Opera companies around the United States and the world have performed the opera since its debut.

It's just one more way of spreading the story that God had Sr. Helen witness on April 5, 1984.

The spirit of *Dead Man Walking* transforms people and stayed with Sarandon and Robbins. Sarandon continues to be an anti-death penalty activist, often partnering with Sr. Helen to fight for the wrongly convicted on death row. She's also appeared on panels about reforming the criminal justice system and narrated documentaries about prisoners on death row who were wrongly convicted.

For his part, in addition to continuing his work with Sr. Helen on the Dead Man Walking School Theatre Project, Robbins developed, with fellow actor Sabra Williams, an arts program for inmates in California's prisons through the Actors' Gang theater group, of which he is the founding artistic director. The Actors' Gang Prison Project, which started in 2010, is an eight-week course for inmates that gives them a chance to transform their emotional lives through acting out their emotions in a safe environment. It also helps them to recognize emotions other people may be feeling in response to their actions.

The mixed-race sessions focus on acting out the heightened emotions of happiness, anger, sadness, and fear. In prisons, inmates tend to segregate themselves by race so the course forces them to interact. Using masks or white face-like mimes, the men and women in prison act and improvise scenes in high emotions. This experience transforms them.

In a 2016 interview with the BBC, Robbins said, "A study came back last December that shows that for those men who took the acting class, there is an 89 percent reduction in infractions, fights within prison, which is huge for the safety of the prison itself and the safety of the corrections officers. They have to deal with a lot less from the people who have been through our program."

He cited another preliminary study, which found that California's 60 percent recidivism rate was cut in half for alumni of the Actors' Gang Prison Project.[13]

"That is the key to rehabilitation, that they stay out of prison. And we now have the evidence that our program does that," Robbins told the BBC.[14]

Every time Sr. Helen gives a talk about the death penalty, she holds up a copy of the book *Dead Man Walking* and says, "Lloyd LeBlanc is the hero of this book." It is not about her. She says she is a storyteller who made a bad mistake. That mistake was not reaching out to the victims' families while she was the spiritual director for Patrick Sonnier. Figuring her presence would only add to their pain, she stayed away. It was the wrong thing to do, she later learned.

In the end, Lloyd LeBlanc approached her and a friendship formed; he taught her that forgiveness is first and foremost not letting one's own life be overcome by hatred.

The two first spoke during a break at Pat's pardon board hearing in Baton Rouge on March 31, 1984. The Bourques, whose daughter Loretta was murdered and raped by the Sonnier brothers, were furious when they saw Sr. Helen. They averted their gaze and walked past her in silence. Lloyd and Eula LeBlanc were right behind them. The first words out of her mouth to them were, "I'm so sorry about your son."

"Sister, I'm a Catholic," Lloyd replied, asking her how she could stand up for Pat without ever visiting him and his wife, Eula, or the Bourques. "How can you spend all your time worrying about Sonnier and not think that maybe we needed you too?" Sr. Helen recalled in *Dead Man Walking*.[15]

At that moment she realized that by not visiting the victims' families, she had hurt them anyway. Lloyd didn't let

Sr. Helen off the hook. Instead, he shared with her his wife's struggles grieving for her son David for days, months, and years on end. Lloyd also shared a side of Pat she never met—a bad man who stole, drank too much, and raped women. The two talked for more than an hour.

It never occurred to Sr. Helen that victims' families might not want the death penalty for their family member's murderer. Neither did she consider that others might pressure the victim's families to push for the death penalty. This was something Lloyd shared with her.

People told Lloyd that if he and his wife said publicly that they didn't want Pat to be executed, it would look like they didn't love their son. Lloyd turned to the church for guidance, but never heard opposition to the death penalty preached from the pulpit. "Sister, you weren't there for us," he told her.

Deep down he felt Jesus would not want them to push for the death of his son's murderer. "Jesus talked to us about forgiving our enemies," Lloyd told Sr. Helen. "People think forgiveness is weak, like you're condoning what the person did. And you didn't really love your son. You don't seem to care because you forgive them. But I don't see it as weakness. I see it as my own life."[16]

He also shared that early on he would imagine himself killing both Pat and Eddie. He pictured himself pulling the switch for the electric chair and seeing them in pain. But the grief and the bitterness began turning Lloyd into an angry person, and he didn't like it. "I'm snapping at Eula. I see pain all around me. I almost lost my wife who almost died of grief and the loss of David. And here I am. I was getting angry, and I was losing who I was because I've always been a kind person who loves to help people," Sr. Helen recalls him saying.[17]

While Lloyd was talking to Sr. Helen during the pardon board hearing that day, he put his hand out, palm faced outward like "stop," and told her, "I said to myself, 'Uh-uh. They killed our son but I'm not going to let them kill me.'" Lloyd decided to embrace grace and Jesus and found himself able to forgive Pat and Eddie. That is why Sr. Helen calls him the hero of *Dead Man Walking.*

"I feel I am still right to oppose capital punishment, but I had not thought seriously enough about what murder means to victims' families and to society," she wrote in *Dead Man Walking.* "I had not considered how difficult the issue of capital punishment is. My response had been far too simplistic."[18]

Lloyd and Sr. Helen stayed in touch after the pardon board hearing, talking on the phone and writing notes to each other. Eventually Sr. Helen visited their home in St. Martinville, Louisiana. At one point in their burgeoning friendship, Lloyd invited Sr. Helen to join him for a holy hour he kept before the Blessed Sacrament from 4:00 a.m. to 5:00 a.m. on Fridays. She agreed and while there, the two prayed the Sorrowful Mysteries of the rosary. It was during this time that Sr. Helen says she had her first real glimpse of what was in Lloyd LeBlanc's heart. He prayed not only for the safety of teenage kids and their families but also for Mrs. Sonnier, Pat and Eddie Sonnier's mother, who lived in a little town and endured the hatred of the community. Townspeople would often make snide comments to her at the grocery store, loud enough so she could hear, and some even threw dead animals on her front porch. When you legalize hatred through something like the death penalty, how do you say to the townspeople, "Don't hate the mother."

Through her friendship with Lloyd, Sr. Helen also realized she needed to do something for victims' families and established an assistance program.

Lloyd wasn't the only family member of a victim opposed to putting the murderer to death. Two such family members share their views in *The Culture of Life and the Death Penalty,* a booklet produced by the US Conference of Catholic Bishops. Mary Bosco Van Valkenburg's brother and sister-in-law were murdered, but no one in her family wanted their killer executed.

"We felt instinctively that vengeance wouldn't alleviate our grief. We wanted this murderer in prison so he could never hurt another person. But wishing he would suffer and die would only have diminished us and shriveled our own souls. Hatred doesn't heal," Van Valkenburg said. "Every time the state kills a person, human society moves in the direction of its lowest, most base urges. We don't have to make that choice."[19]

Bud Welch, father of Julie Welch, who was killed in the 1995 Oklahoma City bombing, also opposed the death penalty for her daughter's murderer. "My conviction is simple: More violence is not what Julie would have wanted. More violence will not bring Julie back. More violence only makes our society more violent," he said.[20]

Victims' families continue to inspire Sr. Helen in her vocation as a witness to state-sanctioned killing. Many people, when they hear of an unspeakable crime, might feel that the perpetrator deserves to die. But they aren't there to see the execution. "It's easy to kill somebody when you think of a monster, an animal," Sr. Helen says. "But it's really hard to kill a human being, and that's part of the story that's in *Dead Man Walking.*"[21]

CHAPTER FIVE

The Death of Innocents

After working for many years with inmates on death row and looking into the details of their trials, Sr. Helen began to notice patterns of abuse and injustice in the legal system that resulted in innocent people being put to death. She wrote about this in her 2005 book *The Death of Innocents: The Eyewitness Account of Wrongful Executions*.

According to the Death Penalty Information Center, 159 people on death row were exonerated as of June 2017. Before she started ministering to those on death row, Sr. Helen believed that the United States had the best court system in the world. Now she knows differently. She also knows that just because one is a faith-filled person doesn't mean one's beliefs are just. For example, Southern states in the Bible Belt have historically and continue to impose the death penalty most often and make up the majority of all executions.

In *The Death of Innocents* Sr. Helen featured the cases of two men—Dobie Gillis Williams and Joseph Roger O'Dell III. Based on evidence and how their cases had been handled by the justice system, she believes they were innocent of the crimes of which they were convicted. Both men were poor, indigent, accused of killing white people, and had inadequate defenses. Sure, each had run-ins with the law before, but that didn't mean they were guilty of these particular crimes.

Dobie was on death row at the Louisiana State Penitentiary in Angola and was the fifth person Sr. Helen accompanied. Dobie faced the same death chamber where Patrick Sonnier was executed, but instead of the electric chair, lethal injection was now the means of execution.

Dobie was a black man with an IQ of 65 (below the level of 70, when someone is considered to have a mental disability). When arrested for murder, he was home for the weekend on furlough from a minimum-security detention facility where he was serving time for burglary. Prison officials allowed him the furlough because he was a model, nonviolent prisoner.

On July 8, 1984, Sonja Merritt Knippers, a forty-three-year-old white woman from Many, Louisiana, was stabbed to death in her bathroom. Her husband, Herb, was home at the time and told police he heard her yell, "A black man is killing me." In response to the husband's information, police arrested three black men on suspicion of her murder. Sister Helen wrote:

> At 2:30 a.m., police officers seized Dobie, asleep on the couch at his grandfather's house, brought him to the police station and began interrogating him. They told him that they would be there for the rest of the night and all morning and all the next day if need be, until they 'got to the bottom of this.' Three police officers later testified that Dobie confessed, and at the crime scene investigators found a bloodstain on a bathroom curtain, which the state crime lab declared was consistent in seven categories with Dobie's, and statistically, that combination would occur in

only two in one hundred thousand black people. Investigators also found a 'dark-pigmented piece of skin' on the brick ledge of the bathroom window, through which the killer supposedly entered and escaped.[1]

Prosecutors said evidence pointed to Dobie's guilt, but Dobie said he was out drinking that night and went home to sleep it off. Dobie's trial lasted one week, and an all-white jury convicted him in 1985 and sentenced him to death.

He sat on death row for fourteen years and was scheduled for execution eleven times before he was finally executed on January 8, 1999. He was thirty-eight.

When Sr. Helen began researching Dobie's case, she noticed information that didn't add up. Dobie's attorney at the trial failed to obtain independent testing of the evidence, which was standard practice, and accepted the prosecution's determination without question. At the crime scene, blood spatters from Sonja's eight stab wounds were everywhere, and yet police couldn't find any blood on Dobie's clothes or body. The prosecution maintained he fled through a small window in the bathroom, but no fingerprints or blood were found there.

While Dobie was on death row, attorneys from the Loyola Death Penalty Resource Center (now closed) began investigating his case and hired bloodstain expert Stuart James to analyze the evidence. Using photos from the crime scene, James said that there was no way someone could stab a person eight times, causing lots of blood splatters, without getting blood all over oneself. The killer also couldn't spring up and vault through the small bathroom window without leaving fingerprints behind. Furthermore, no footprints were found in the bathroom or outside the window. The killer had to leave through the bathroom door, James said. Sonja's husband, Herb, was never questioned by the prosecution at trial or investigated by police as a possible suspect. It was just one more thing that didn't add up.

Attorneys and investigators for Dobie found missing evidence, questionable forensic testing, and other information that raised serious questions about his guilt—including one judge selecting a questionable lab to conduct DNA testing. But the team could not secure his freedom.

Sister Helen visited Dobie for eight years prior to his execution, and they corresponded regularly outside of her visits to Angola.

Unlike Pat Sonnier's handwriting, which was in cursive and heavily slanted to the left with small letters, Dobie's handwriting looked more like that of a teenager's with upright characters in cursive and smiley faces after a sentence when he wanted to make Sr. Helen laugh.

Sister Helen's letters to Dobie are in the archive at DePaul University in Chicago. She was a faithful correspondent, writing to Dobie at least once or twice a month. Her relationship with Dobie coincided with the making of the movie *Dead Man Walking* and its national and international release. The events were chronicled through Dobie's and Sr. Helen's letters.

On March 5, 1994, Dobie responded to Sr. Helen's letter to him that included a photo taken on the set of the movie. The photo cut off half of Susan Sarandon's face, and Sr. Helen apologized. "And it doesn't matter that part of her face was cut off by that car door, so don't sweat it, okay? Okay!" Dobie wrote, adding a small smiley face after the sentence.[2]

It turned out the death row inmate also collected autographs. "Sister Helen, I really am looking forward to receiving both Susan Sarandon's and Tim Robbins' autographs, plus that personal note you mentioned; and I want you to know that I'll always be grateful to you for doing this for me! When I receive their autographs, I'll then have three famous people's autographs—yours and theirs!" he wrote on February 14, 1994.[3]

On March 4, 1996, Sr. Helen wrote to Dobie about the Academy Award nominations for the film *Dead Man Walking.*

"Did you hear about our four Academy Award nominations for the film? Susan, Sean, and Tim. Tim was really a surprise—best director nomination and this was only his second movie," she wrote, adding that Bruce Springsteen received a nomination for best original song.

Dobie replied: "So Bruce Springsteen got an Oscar award nomination for best original song, huh? Well, I think that's really great!!"

Sister Helen often sent him postcards from her travels. She also did that with other inmates and was a faithful correspondent. Each letter was important because she understood they were starving for interaction outside of the prison walls. Sometimes Dobie and the other inmates Sr. Helen visited asked for basic things like underwear, pajamas, and tennis shoes. They didn't have any income on death row so were beholden to others. All of the requests were for basic things people on the outside took for granted, including good writing implements. "I really appreciate those good ink pens that you gave me at the seminar! These ink pens that the classification officers issue to us are really sorry," Dobie wrote.[4]

But corresponding with people on the outside came with a sense of loss when their pen pals stopped writing. Dobie mentioned this a few times in his letters. "Sometimes I feel like maybe after all these years of being on death row and in prison, the people that I've been corresponding with over the years (including family members) just get tired of writing, and decide not to write me for quite a while, and some of my pen pals just stopped writing altogether! I'm sure that absence really does make the heart grow fonder but too much absence will make one wonder. I can't hold it against them, however, because after all nobody's under any obligation to write to me!" Dobie wrote on July 15, 1994.[5]

Like other inmates before him, Dobie drew pictures on his letters and envelopes. On March 7, 1996, he drew a large sunshine in yellow marker with a smiling face on the letter, along with flowers and trees on the other pages. "Although you seem to be a naturally cheerful person, I just thought I'd draw a few pictures for you, in this letter, and color them, with the hope that they'll help to add to your cheerfulness!" he wrote.[6]

While Dobie was on death row, Sr. Helen was lobbying for the end to the death penalty, so reporters around the country interviewed him. One reporter had upset him, and he wrote to Sr. Helen about it. The reporter had asked him if he felt any remorse for killing Knippers. "I thought it really unfair of her to have asked me such a question as that, because for her to have asked me something like that just let me know that she just assumed that I'm guilty, without ever having asked me first, whether or not I'm guilty, but at the same time, I was glad that she did ask me that as it gave me a chance to clarify that point; I was most sincere when I told her that (because I DIDN'T kill Mrs. Knippers). I don't/can't feel any remorse, but that I can only empathize and sympathize with them (the Knippers family) because I too have a mother and that I know how I'd feel if something like that was to happen to her."[7]

Like with others whom Sr. Helen corresponded, Dobie often told her he couldn't put into words how much her visits meant to him. They meant a good deal to Sr. Helen as well. On one occasion in February of 1996, bad weather forced Sr. Helen to leave the prison before seeing Dobie. "It was TERRIBLE being so close to you there at Angola but having to leave before I could see you because of the freezing roads. That was a <u>first</u> which I hope will never be repeated. . . . I want to reschedule our visit NEXT WEEK," she wrote on February 5, 1996.[8]

Sr. Helen even developed the habit of drawing her own pictures on her letters to Dobie. Even though he was executed in 1999, his correspondence to Sr. Helen ended in 1996, possibly due to an onset of rheumatoid arthritis.

By the time of his execution, the arthritis had taken over his body, gnarling his hands and causing great pain in his left knee. In his last hours, Dobie phoned family members telling them he was grateful for their support along the way. "I have noticed this same spirit of gratefulness in every person I have accompanied in this bizarre death process," Sr. Helen wrote.[9]

In the death chamber after they hooked up the IVs that would administer the killing cocktail, the warden asked Dobie if he had any last words. "I just want to say I got no hard feelings for anybody. God bless everybody. God bless," Dobie said.[10] What's the official cause of death written on the death certificate? Homicide.

While Dobie was on death row, Sr. Helen corresponded with Feltus Taylor, another inmate on the tier with Dobie. She wasn't his spiritual advisor and visited him only periodically after he reached out to her. Unlike Dobie, Feltus admitted to committing the murder he had been convicted of—killing a former coworker as he robbed his former workplace in Baton Rouge, Louisiana. He also shot his former boss and permanently paralyzed him. Feltus plead guilty to the crime.

Feltus was on death row when Dobie was executed and wrote to Sr. Helen offering condolences. "Well, I'm sorry that you lost Dobie on Friday night. I know it must be hard on you and his family," he wrote on January 11, 1999.

Feltus said he felt down and then up on Friday because he knew that all of Dobie's struggles were now over. "And sometimes I wish that it was me instead of him because a lot of times I wish all of this stuff was just over with, you know." But Feltus was also curious about the process of execution as someone headed for the same fate and wrote: "How does it makes you feel when you sit and look at something like that? Did he look to be okay with everything? Did he look like he was in pain while it was going on? It's so hard to think you'll be alive, then all of the life is taken away from you in that way."[11]

As only a death-row inmate might wonder, he wrote, "I think about how it must feel to lie on that bed and to know that you want to be getting off of it, have to be hard. But it's what we are faced with every day."

When she first began her ministry to people on death row, Sr. Helen assumed everyone was guilty like Feltus and had received a fair trial. But years of working with prisoners and their attorneys taught her that wasn't always the case, and flaws in the criminal justice system could lead to the conviction of people innocent of the crime in question. They may be guilty of other crimes, but not that one.

Sister Helen also learned that what happens during the trial is crucial to whether or not a person's conviction could be overturned later on, no matter what new evidence was revealed. Virtually no court will revisit material presented at the trial and upon which the jury ruled. "With so much in the balance as you go to trial, you better have a skilled, energetic lawyer who thoroughly knows the law and how to conduct an exhaustive investigation and is aggressive enough to get hold of the original police report with its fresh, uncensored reporting of facts and eyewitness accounts," she wrote in *The Death of Innocents*.[12] Dobie didn't have that defense.

Just four years after Dobie's execution in 2002, the US Supreme Court issued a ruling that would have spared his life. In Atkins v. Virginia, the highest court in the land determined that executing those with mental disabilities, whom they termed "mentally retarded," (an IQ of 70 or lower) violated the Eighth Amendment banning "cruel and unusual punishment."

Dobie's death rekindled the fire burning within Sr. Helen to witness to these injustices. She promised Dobie before he died that she would tell his story, and she did in *The Death of Innocents*. In that same book, she also told the story of Joseph Roger O'Dell III.

Sister Helen was pulled into Joseph's case by Lori Urs, a volunteer at a Virginia Innocence Project who, with investigators, looked into his case and found a large amount of exculpatory evidence kept from the jury in his trial.

Joseph, a white male out on parole, was convicted of the murder, rape, and sodomy of Helen Schartner, a forty-four-year-old secretary who was bludgeoned and strangled to death after she left a Virginia Beach nightclub on February 5, 1985. Joseph had also visited the club that night. The next day, after hearing about the murder, Joseph's girlfriend and landlord called the police saying she found his bloody clothes in a garbage can. Crime lab testing said the blood on his clothing was similar to the victim's and arrested him.

Joseph maintained that the blood on his clothes came from a fight he was in the night of the murder. While he did visit the club where Schartner was last seen, he visited other bars too—getting into a fight outside one of them—and didn't get to his girlfriend's home until 7:00 a.m. the next morning. Despite being assigned an attorney by the court, Joseph chose to represent himself at trial. When Sr. Helen learned of this by reading documents Lori Urs had sent her, she wondered why the court let him do it. She also wondered later how "every court in the land would fail to render a judgment of ineffectiveness of counsel."[13]

Joseph said he didn't trust his attorney so he fired him. Through her investigation, Lori found that this attorney withheld exculpatory evidence from Joseph from the outset. During the trial, the prosecution presented its forensic evidence and expert witnesses saying Joseph, who had served time previously for other crimes, was guilty. They also produced Joseph's cellmate at the time of his arrest who said Joseph confessed to the killing. Joseph was convicted and sentenced to death at Mecklenberg Prison in Boydton, Virginia.

Joseph did have a violent past. He had served time in Florida for attempted kidnapping and later killed a fellow inmate while serving time for a different crime in a Virginia prison. But Sr. Helen didn't believe he murdered Schartner.

Often people who are innocent believe all they have to do is tell their story and a jury will believe them. That was true in Joseph's case. What they don't anticipate is how the prosecution's job is to get a conviction, and how the prosecution will do everything they can to make that happen. With 159 death-row prisoners exonerated at the time of this book's printing, Sr. Helen hears more and more stories of just what the prosecution will do to ensure that their version of the crime prevails—even if the person is innocent. Personal ambition or politics can play a part in how aggressive the prosecution is to get a conviction.

Sometimes the injustice seems to be rooted in arrogance, such as when the Virginia Supreme Court—"whose task it is to make sure that a petitioner's constitutional rights are respected during trial,"[14] Sr. Helen recounted—refused to hear Joseph's petition on account of word choice. His lawyers typed "Notice of Appeal" on the title page of his petition instead of "Petition for Appeal." Two words made the court not hear the case of a man the state wanted to kill. "To what level of moral bankruptcy has the judiciary system fallen that a court can do this to a man scheduled to be killed by the state?" Sr. Helen wondered.[15]

Joseph's experiences reminded Sr. Helen of Dobie's trial. "The prosecutors wove a preposterous and convoluted scenario of the crime in which Dobie was the only possible culprit, while the victim's husband, who was alone in the house with his wife when she was murdered, was never investigated as a possible suspect. Moreover, Dobie's alleged confession was attested to by two policemen, who claimed to have 'lost' the tape on which Dobie confessed. And both Dobie and Joe had previous records, making it easy to believe they could have committed the crimes. They were easy targets," she wrote.[16]

After six years in prison, Joseph used the writ of habeas corpus to ask the US Supreme Court to grant him an evidentiary hearing where he could present DNA testing that contradicted the claim that the blood on his clothes was consistent with the victim's. Every US citizen is guaranteed the writ of habeas corpus, which asks a federal court to determine if a state's imprisonment of a person is lawful.

While the Supreme Court in 1991 decided not to hear Joseph's petition, Justices Harry Blackmun, John Paul Stevens, and Sandra Day O'Connor issued a statement saying that there were serious questions about Joseph's guilt and his ability to represent himself at trial. "Because of the gross injustice that would result if an innocent man were sentenced to death,

O'Dell's substantial federal claims can and should receive careful consideration from the federal court with habeas corpus jurisdiction over the case," the statement read.[17]

Joseph finally had his evidentiary hearing, and a federal judge ruled in his favor, saying the blood on his shirt and jacket were not a conclusive match to the victim's. However, in 1996, the Fourth Circuit Court said it was irrelevant that the bloodstains didn't match, essentially shutting down the DNA angle.

Another thing that Sr. Helen learned on her journey with Joseph was that district attorneys, often with the hope of furthering their careers, frequently do not tell juries that instead of the death penalty, they can choose life without parole for the accused. Most juries do not want putting someone to death on their consciences. But they also want to ensure that the perpetrator cannot be put back out on the streets. Studies show that when life without parole is an option, the number of death sentences drops.

The US Supreme Court ruled in 1994 that in some cases juries must be told that they can sentence a person to life without parole. Since this was not the case during Joseph's sentencing, his lawyers petitioned the court to consider that aspect of his case, but they ruled it was not retroactive to his case. Joseph once again asked the state of Virginia to conduct DNA tests on other pieces of evidence to demonstrate his innocence, but the state refused. Joseph's execution date was set for July 23, 1997 at 9:00 p.m.

During the time that Joseph and Lori visited, wrote letters, and worked together, they fell in love and decided to marry. This changed her status at the prison from paralegal working on his case to girlfriend. There were more restrictions on visits by girlfriends. The day before his execution, Lori and

Sr. Helen visited with Joseph. The wedding was scheduled for the following afternoon, but Lori worried prison officials wouldn't allow her to return. As his spiritual advisor Sr. Helen could make a return visit in the evening. During that time she delivered a personal message to Joseph from Mother Teresa. The nun from Kolkata also called Virginia Governor George Allen on Joseph's behalf saying killing was wrong, and it was against God's commandments, no matter who or why they were doing it. That cheered Joseph, and they prayed together.

The last days and hours are always tense, and the condemned and his family get little sleep, Sr. Helen says. "The one thing I know about making it through these last days and hours is that grace never comes ahead of time, it unfurls under you as you need it."[18]

On the afternoon of his execution date, Lori and Joseph married in a brief death house ceremony. Prison staff strip-searched both Lori and Sr. Helen before they entered the death house. Once inside, the minister, Sr. Helen, Joseph, and Lori formed a circle during the ceremony; both the minister and Sr. Helen held Joseph and Lori's hands because the two weren't allowed to touch. The newlyweds were allowed to visit together for a time, but then Sr. Helen and Lori had to leave. Sister Helen could return later.

At 4:00 p.m. they learned that Governor Allen refused Joseph's petition for clemency. Only a stay from the US Supreme Court could save him. Sister Helen and his lawyers headed back to the prison to be with Joseph. From where she sat in the death house, she could see the death chamber and the gurney through a window. "There it is, cross-shaped, with arms angled downward—Joe O'Dell's modern, high-tech crucifix. It has a lot of straps, folded neatly across the top of the gurney," she wrote.[19]

Sister Helen was allowed into the death chamber with Joseph while guards strapped him down. Then she moved to a room next door where witnesses would watch the execution through glass. "A guard holds the telephone for Joe to say his last words: 'This is the happiest day of my life. I married Lori today,' " Sr. Helen recalls Joseph saying. He also told Governor Allen he was killing an innocent man and apologized to the victim's son. "Eddie Schartner, I'm sorry about your mother, but I didn't kill her. I hope you find out the truth." And finally he said, "Lori, I will love you through eternity."[20]

In 1996 the people of Italy, who are largely against the death penalty, became interested in Joseph's case—even Pope John Paul II weighed in. On the night of Joseph's execution, an estimated five million people in Italy stayed up until 3:00 a.m. to hear of Joseph's fate. An Italian parliament member had invited Lori to speak around the country about Joseph's case. After his death in 1997, the town of Palermo, Italy, paid to transport Joseph's body to its city for burial. Sister Helen and Lori traveled with the body, but before reaching Palermo they stopped in Rome for an impromptu private meeting with Pope John Paul II.

In a comic moment, Sr. Helen looked at what she was wearing and panicked. She couldn't meet the Holy Father wearing pants. "In a small parlor, right next to the large room where the pope will come to meet us, I accomplish the quickest change of clothes in my life." She donned panty-hose, which were uncooperative in the summer heat, a blouse, skirt, and her cross around her neck. But the chain of the cross snapped, so she tied the chain in a knot, threw it over her head, and ran to the next room. What about her hair? "Forget the hair, the pope doesn't give a hoot about women's hair," she told herself.[21]

A few minutes later, Pope John Paul II shuffled in. He looked very tired, Sr. Helen recalls. "He walks right up to us, to Lori first, takes her hand in his, and says, 'I prayed for Joseph at Mass,'" Sr. Helen wrote in *The Death of Innocents*. Sister Helen reached out her hand to him and thanked him for speaking out against the death penalty and for helping the church embrace opposition to it. "He nods, blesses me, and kisses me on the forehead. The burdens that he carries are written in his face and his stooped shoulders. As he turns to leave, I say to him, 'Take care of yourself.'"[22]

That was her first meeting with a pope, but not her first interaction with Pope John Paul II.

CHAPTER SIX

The Church and the Death Penalty

In February 2016, Pope Francis called for a moratorium on the death penalty during the Jubilee of Mercy, which ended in November 2016. He said the commandment "Thou shalt not kill," applied to the guilty as well as the innocent. The Catholic Church has not always spoken so boldly and clearly against the death penalty. But Sr. Helen helped change that practice with a letter to Pope John Paul II in January of 1997. That letter influenced change in the church's teaching on the death penalty as outlined in the Catechism of the Catholic Church.

In 1997 Lori Urs, the volunteer who assisted and married death-row inmate Joseph O'Dell, invited Sr. Helen to accompany her on a speaking tour of Italy. Italian Parliament member Luciano Neri had invited Lori to speak in various cities about O'Dell's case. The Italian people were captured by O'Dell's case and lobbied for him. *Dead Man Walking* was a success in Italy, and Lori told Sr. Helen the Italian Parliament was arranging a visit to the Vatican with a possible meeting with John Paul II.

That same year, Sr. Helen received an invitation to meet the pope in person at the Vatican with some anti-death penalty lawyers, but declined to go because her closest friend was dying. Instead, she drafted a letter on January 1, and the lawyers delivered it to someone from the Holy See's Secretariat of State, who handed it directly to the pontiff on January 22.

"They said the pope read every word of your letter," Sr. Helen recalls.[1]

John Paul II had just been given the final draft of the second edition of the Catechism of the Catholic Church, the universal tool that outlines the church's beliefs and is used for teaching those beliefs around the world. He was reviewing it for approval. Two years prior, in 1995, John Paul II had released *Evangelium Vitae* (The Gospel of Life), an encyclical letter—a document promulgated by popes that carries the most weight in terms of importance—on the church's teaching on the sanctity of human life. In this encyclical he left a door open for use of the death penalty. He wrote:

> There is a growing tendency, both in the Church and in civil society, to demand that [the death penalty] be applied in a very limited way or even that it be abolished completely. The problem must be viewed in the context of a system of penal justice ever more in line with human dignity and thus, in the end, with God's plan for man and society. The primary purpose of the punishment which society inflicts is "to redress the disorder caused by the offence." Public authority must redress the violation of personal and social rights by imposing on the offender an adequate punishment for the crime, as a condition for the offender to regain the exercise of his or her freedom. In this way authority also fulfils the purpose of defending public order and ensuring people's safety, while at the same

time offering the offender an incentive and help to change his or her behavior and be rehabilitated.

It is clear that, for these purposes to be achieved, the nature and extent of the punishment must be carefully evaluated and decided upon, and ought not go to the extreme of executing the offender except in cases of absolute necessity: in other words, when it would not be possible otherwise to defend society. Today however, as a result of steady improvements in the organization of the penal system, such cases are very rare, if not practically non-existent.

In any event, the principle set forth in the new Catechism of the Catholic Church remains valid: "If bloodless means are sufficient to defend human lives against an aggressor and to protect public order and the safety of persons, public authority must limit itself to such means, because they better correspond to the concrete conditions of the common good and are more in conformity to the dignity of the human person."[2]

John Paul II had pushed the death penalty to the very edge and said, if we have a way to keep society safe, which we do, we don't need to resort to killing. The death penalty should be rare if not nonexistent. However, Sr. Helen saw those words as a way for people to support the death penalty because they would quote the pope and say, "Well, he didn't rule it out altogether."

In her letter to John Paul II, Sr. Helen explained that his words would be "quoted to death" and that governments would always claim it's an "absolute necessity to kill the person."[3] She was right. In her home state of Louisiana, New Orleans district attorney Harry Connick Sr. quoted the pope's words during a BBC interview.

She also questioned John Paul II on the dignity of the death of the one killed. In the United States and beyond, those subjected to the death penalty were often rendered defenseless ahead of time. In the case of those executed in the United States, prior to their death officials moved them to a waiting room near the "death chamber," as Sr. Helen called it, with the lights on twenty-four hours a day in a room with no windows and little contact with the outside world. They were defenseless. "Where is the dignity in this death?" Sr. Helen wrote. "It's the intentional killing of some-one rendered defenseless."

"What all of the men I have accompanied (three) have said when at last they died was, 'I am so tired.' Conscious human beings anticipate death and die a thousand times before they die, no matter what the 'humane' method of death may be, even lethal injection, which is supposed to just 'put you to sleep,' " she wrote to the pope.[4]

Governments can't be trusted to be fair in deciding whom to execute, she told John Paul II. "From the time of St. Augustine of Hippo, one of the first to argue that the 'wicked' might be 'coerced with the sword,' we Catholics have upheld the right of governments to take life in defense of the common good. But, as you point out in *Evangelium Vitae*, the development in societies of penal institutions now offers a way for societies to protect themselves from violent offenders without imitating the very violence they claim to abhor . . . How can any government, vulnerable to undue influence of the rich and powerful and subject to every kind of prejudice, have the purity and integrity to select certain of its citizens for punishment by death?"[5]

She also laid out the emphasis of prosecutors on the poor when seeking the death penalty.

"The vast majority of people on death row in the U.S.—85 percent—are chosen for death because they killed white people; whereas when people of color are killed (fully 50 percent of all homicides) not only is the death penalty seldom sought, but often there is not even vigorous prosecution of such cases."[6]

Seeing the faces of the condemned and watching them die made their humanity all too apparent, she wrote to the pope. "'I just pray that God holds up my legs,' each one of the condemned said to me as they were about to walk to their deaths, and from the depths of my soul, from Christ burning within me, I found myself saying to them, 'Look at me. Look at my face. I will be the face of Christ for you.'"[7]

Shortly after her letter reached John Paul II, Sr. Helen received word that the Holy See delayed publication of the second edition of the Catechism because there was something about the death penalty. "I went, 'No! It couldn't be happening! Is it possible?'"[8]

Indeed it was possible.

When the Catechism came out, this is what it said regarding the death penalty:

> Assuming that the guilty party's identity and responsibility have been fully determined, the traditional teaching of the Church does not exclude recourse to the death penalty, if this is the only possible way of effectively defending human lives against the unjust aggressor.
>
> If, however, non-lethal means are sufficient to defend and protect people's safety from the aggressor, authority will limit itself to such means, as these are more in keeping with the concrete conditions of the common good and more in conformity with the dignity of the human person.
>
> Today, in fact, as a consequence of the possibilities which the state has for effectively preventing crime, by rendering one who has committed an offense incapable of doing harm—without definitively taking away from him the possibility of redeeming himself—the cases in which the

execution of the offender is an absolute necessity "are very rare, if not practically non-existent" (John Paul II, *Evangelium Vitae* 56).[9]

John Paul II removed the reference to allowing capital punishment for "grave and grievous crimes." Sister Helen was thrilled.

When John Paul II visited St. Louis in 1999, he again called for an end to the death penalty. During his homily on January 27 in the Trans World Dome in St. Louis he said, "A sign of hope is the increasing recognition that the dignity of human life must never be taken away, even in the case of someone who has done great evil. Modern society has the means of protecting itself, without definitively denying criminals the chance to reform. I renew the appeal I made most recently at Christmas for a consensus to end the death penalty, which is both cruel and unnecessary."[10]

Some years earlier the Catholics bishops in the United States had begun backing away from full support of the death penalty. In 1974 the US Conference of Catholic Bishops released a statement saying, "by a substantial majority, [we] voted to declare its opposition to capital punishment."

In 1980 the US bishops' conference released another statement on capital punishment that further questioned its use. They nodded to church teaching allowing for states to decide over the executions, but questioned whether conditions exist for it in modern society. Taking a life denies the offender an opportunity to reform, and studies have not "given conclusive evidence that would justify the imposition of the death penalty on a few individuals as a means of preventing others from committing crimes," the bishops wrote.

They continued, "Abolition of the death penalty shows society that we believe that the cycle of violence can be broken; that every person is unique and valuable in the eyes of God—no matter what their transgressions; that only God has the right to take a life; and that it mirrors most of the teaching of Jesus. However, in the same paragraph as the last point, the bishops pointed to early Church teaching that said Christians could be involved in executing the offenders as long as they weren't ministers of the Church."[11]

In the 1980 statement, the bishops even acknowledged flaws in administering the death penalty, such as biases and racism inherent to the US legal system, but especially the chance for that system to make a mistake.

"Because death terminates the possibilities of conversion and growth and support that we can share with each other, we regard a mistaken infliction of the death penalty with a special horror, even while we retain our trust in God's loving mercy," the bishops wrote.

Death penalty trials involve lengthy appeals, which hurt both the families of victims and the accused. In the end it doesn't benefit anyone. They continued: "We believe that the actual carrying out of the death penalty brings with it great and avoidable anguish for the criminal, for his family and loved ones, and for those who are called on to perform or to witness the execution."[12]

In 2005 the US Conference of Catholic Bishops released *A Culture of Life and the Penalty of Death*, a definitive teaching document outlining the church's evolved thinking relating to the death penalty after St. John Paul II's changes in the Catechism. That same year, the conference launched its "Campaign to End the Use of the Death Penalty." In 2015 the bishops called for a recommitment to this campaign: "We renew our common conviction that it is time for our nation to abandon the illusion that we can protect life by taking life," which the bishops had written in *A Culture of Life and the Penalty of Death*.

The document left the door open to execute on some occasions. In Catholic teaching the state has the recourse to impose the death penalty upon criminals convicted of heinous crimes if this ultimate sanction is the only available means to protect society from a grave threat to human life. However, this right should not be exercised when other ways are available to punish criminals and to protect society, which are more respectful of human life.

Eventually, the bishops come to the same conclusion about the death penalty as Sr. Helen—ultimately it's about us, "the actions taken in our name, the values which guide our lives, and the dignity that we accord to human life. Public policies that treat some lives as unworthy of protection, or that are perceived as vengeful, fracture the moral conviction that human life is sacred."[13]

If there has been any doubt about the Catholic Church's support for abolishing the death penalty, John Paul II's successors Benedict XVI and Francis have removed it. Frequently in his brief pontificate, Pope Benedict called on countries around the world to end use of the death penalty.

In his first pastoral visit to the United States in 2015, Pope Francis addressed a joint session of the US Congress—the first pope ever to do so—and in his remarks he advocated for an end to the death penalty. "The Golden Rule also reminds us of our responsibility to protect and defend human life at every stage of its development," Pope Francis told Congress on September 24, 2015. "This conviction has led me, from the beginning of my ministry, to advocate at different levels for the global abolition of the death penalty. I am convinced that this way is the best, since every life is sacred, every human person is endowed with an inalienable dignity, and society can only benefit from the rehabilitation of those convicted of crimes."[14]

He also cheered the US Catholic bishops' renewed commitment to this cause and offered his moral support to others working in the abolitionist movement. He has also reached out personally to governors asking for them to grant clemency to death-row inmates.

Sister Helen met Pope Francis at the Vatican on January 21, 2016, and delivered a thank-you letter from Richard Glossip, whose execution in the United States was halted in September 2015. Pope Francis reached out to Oklahoma Governor Mary Fallin asking her not to execute Richard. After the meeting, Sr. Helen said it was "the highlight of my life."

Sister Helen's work with death-row inmate Richard Glossip began when he called her on January 5, 2015, asking her to attend his execution, which was scheduled a few weeks later on January 29.

Richard, who at the time this book was released, was on death row in Oklahoma and had been convicted of the 1997 murder of Barry Van Treese, the owner of an Oklahoma City hotel where Richard was manager. As of June 2017, Glossip had four stays of execution, and Oklahoma had put a hold on all executions.

Sister Helen, who normally takes only one person on death row at a time and accompanies them to the end, was already accompanying Manuel Ortiz. He was an inmate in the Louisiana State Penitentiary in Angola convicted in 1994 of hiring someone to kill his wife and killing his wife's friend. But she agreed to Richard's request despite not knowing she would make time for him with her busy travel schedule.

After she decided to accompany Richard, she looked into his case and ultimately came to believe he was innocent of the crime. In some instances, district attorneys abuse the discretionary power given to them to pursue the death penalty, using it to further their political career or agendas. Because of that, along with being in a pro-death penalty state like Oklahoma and having an inadequate defense, Sr. Helen believed Richard had been wrongly convicted.

Upon the statement of Justin Sneed, a nineteen-year-old methamphetamine addict, who worked as a handyman at the hotel, Richard was convicted of allegedly offering Sneed money to kill Van Treese. Richard allegedly wanted Van Treese out of the way so he could persuade Van Treese's wife to let him manage both of their motels. He allegedly told Sneed they could also rob Van Treese of the motel money he had on him and split the profits.

The local police kept Sneed in custody for six months without a lawyer and told him he could receive the death penalty if he didn't implicate Richard. In a routine trial, Richard's lawyers would look for evidence to impeach Sneed's credibility. They didn't do that. Instead, Sneed implicated Richard in the murder and robbery, and the jury convicted him. It was solely on Sneed's word that Richard was sentenced to the death penalty. No physical evidence against Richard was produced at the trial.

During a trial the prosecution typically presents forensic evidence found at the scene of the crime. Then the defense presents independent testing of the physical evidence to show why it doesn't connect to their client. However, Richard's defense attorney didn't investigate the evidence. Sister Helen believes the prosecutor and the judge intimidated him. The person on trial, in this case Richard, received a poor defense, either because they were poorly paid, overworked, or they were intimidated by the system; they just stopped raising objections because the judge always opposed the objections of the prosecution but always overruled the defense's objections.

The district attorney who prosecuted Richard's trial pushed for the death penalty in fifty-four other cases. Whenever he would run for office in Oklahoma, he would brag about how many death penalties he got and led voters to think he was fighting for their safety, Sr. Helen says.

After reading the case history, she began putting a team together, finding lawyers—led by attorney Don Knight—who would take on Richard's defense. From past experience she knew Richard needed good lawyers, and that they would have to work his case through the courts. The lawyers began gathering the exculpatory evidence—evidence gathered and presented at a trial that favors the defendant to show he or she is not guilty—that Richard's first lawyers didn't do.

The legal team hired investigators who soon discovered that the police detectives assigned to Sneed had a history of forced confessions. They believed that, in exchange for Sneed's testimony against Richard at trial, these detectives promised Sneed he wouldn't receive the death penalty. The investigators also found people, including Sneed's drug dealer, who would testify that Sneed had a bad meth addiction and that his word wasn't reliable. Sometimes Sneed would buy drugs using change stolen from vending machines or stolen items like a car stereo.

"He was a bad meth addict. He was injecting intravenously. That's all he could think was to get drugs," Sr. Helen says. "But the prosecutor in the closing arguments said Justin [Sneed] might have used drugs every now and then but mostly he was just a loner of a guy who had left home."[15]

Another person the investigators found was a man who was in jail with Sneed after he was first arrested. He told them how scared Sneed was that they would give him the death penalty. Sneed told his cellmate how he went in to rob Van Treese and ended up killing him. According to this witness,

Sneed never mentioned Richard. A third person the investigators found was in jail with him and admitted to overhearing Sneed tell his cellmate about how he committed the crime but the police and prosecutors pinned it on Richard.

Richard appealed his conviction but lost. If during a trial a person doesn't have a lawyer who will raise an objection to something in the process, no appeals court will look at that case. That is the problem of inadequate defense. It damages the process further down the line. A person on trial needs very good lawyers at the outset.

When Sr. Helen decided to help Richard, she didn't just summon lawyers and investigators to his aide. She also summoned her well-known friends like actress Susan Sarandon, who portrayed Sr. Helen in the movie *Dead Man Walking*; TV host Bill Maher; director Tim Robbins who wrote and directed *Dead Man Walking*; and business mogul Richard Branson. Branson even took out two full-page ads in the Oklahoma City newspaper prior to two of Richard's execution dates and called on the state not to kill a man who was probably innocent. Interest in Richard's case also reached beyond US borders, including a five-part series on England's SKYNews.

Leading up to Richard's August 2015 execution date, Sarandon arranged for herself and Sr. Helen to be interviewed on *Dr. Phil*, a popular daily talk show hosted by psychologist Dr. Phil McGraw, who was made famous by Oprah Winfrey. The show was devoted to Richard's case, and was initially scheduled to air on September 8, 2015. However, Sarandon told Dr. Phil that wouldn't work because the date was too close to Richard's next execution date of September 30. She convinced Dr. Phil of the urgency to air the show, and he preempted a scheduled summer break of reruns to air it on August 31. He even gave it a big promotional push. The appeal efforts went viral on social media and people all over the world heard about Richard's case.

Everyone was trying to sway the actions of Oklahoma's Governor Mary Fallin, who was in favor of the death penalty. Even Pope Francis sent her a letter asking her not to execute Richard. Fallin responded saying this had been through the court and she had to abide by the law, which was what the citizens wanted. The efforts of Sr. Helen and others drawing attention to the case outside of the state angered the governor, and she told news media that outsiders wouldn't tell her what she should do.

While the clock was ticking on Richard's next execution date, lawyers were working behind the scenes in the court and with anyone who might know him. When Richard was sentenced to death, Oklahoma had three other men on death row. All four men were slated for immediate execution.

In April 2014 Oklahoma botched the execution of Clayton Lockett, who writhed on the gurney for more than forty-five minutes before dying of a heart attack. When the state resumed executions with Charles Warner in January 2015, they used potassium acetate—not potassium chloride as required under state protocol—and witnesses say he screamed out that his body was on fire.

In recent years, companies stopped producing the drugs used in executions, so states have begun to experiment on new combinations of drugs for lethal injections. There are no regulations or monitoring of how executions are done or what drugs are used.

Charles Warner may have been spared if the US Supreme Court decided a week or two earlier to hear the case Glossip v. Gross, where Warner and the other Oklahoma death-row inmates—Richard Glossip, John Grant, and Benjamin Cole—were attempting to bar the use of the drug midazolam in the cocktail for executions, saying that the sedative didn't work and they would be subjected to extreme pain when the other drugs were administered. The third lethal drug in the cocktail is known to make people feel they are being burned alive. Oklahoma began using midazolam after drug companies in Europe and the United States, pressured by death-penalty abolitionists, refused to sell states the barbiturates used in the past. Charles Warner was executed a week before the court decided to hear the case.

On June 29, 2015, the Supreme Court ruled against the inmates, five to four. But in an historic dissent, Justice Stephen Breyer, joined by Justice Ruth Bader Ginsberg, raised a larger question about state-sanctioned executions. "Rather than try to patch up the death penalty's legal wounds one at a time, I would ask for full briefing on a more basic question: whether the death penalty violates the Constitution." Breyer also wrote, "It is highly likely that the death penalty violates the Eighth Amendment," barring cruel and unusual punishment. It remains to be seen if this case helped pave the way for the end to the death penalty in the United States.[16]

Richard Glossip went to the death house three times anticipating his death. Sister Helen describes the death house as a building made out of cement where the condemned prisoner is taken a few weeks before his execution. The prisoner is confined to a room with no windows and a cement slab for a bed. When she saw Richard there, he had bruises on his hips from trying to sleep on the slab. But sleep doesn't come easily since guards keep the lights on twenty-four hours a day monitoring the condemned for possible suicide attempts.

Richard spent several weeks in this cell, which is located just a few feet away from the death chamber, and lost dozens of pounds. It is a form of torture, Sr. Helen says. "People are conscious and have imaginations. They anticipate dying and have nightmares about being taken and dying over and over again before they actually die. One day as a nation when we wake up we're going to recognize that that's torture."[17]

The night before Richard's scheduled execution on September 30, prison officials shut off his access to visitors and the phone. They ignored the fact that Sr. Helen was his official spiritual advisor and therefore supposed to be allowed to accompany him in his last hours. Richard was supposed to be killed at 3:00 p.m., so Sr. Helen and three of Richard's attorneys were at the prison waiting to be led over to the death chamber.

It got to be 2:30 and Sr. Helen thought the van would be there to take them over to the execution. "I kept looking at my watch," Sr. Helen recalls. "I found a little place in this room where I can just pray—pray for Richard, pray for everybody. I pray, 'God, you know the man is innocent. You really are in charge of every life that comes to you. I just ask you to spare Richard.' "[18] Soon it was 2:45 p.m. and still no van. Finally, at 3:55 p.m. they learned that Governor Fallin issued a stay of execution saying there was a mix-up with the drugs that were to be use for lethal injection.

"Then by the next day they had extended it indefinitely because Richard's case blew the whole thing open," Sr. Helen says.[19] Media digging into the earlier botched executions started detailing what was happening. They reported how the drug used in Charles Warner's execution is used to embalm people after they are dead. That drug changes the liquid composition of a person's body so Warner was mummified alive.

As of June 2017, Richard remained on death row awaiting his fate.

CHAPTER SEVEN

Her Thoughts on the Death Penalty

Since 1984 Sr. Helen has witnessed six executions and has had time to develop her thoughts on the death penalty, which she says first and foremost is about us.

When people ask Sr. Helen how she can minister to and care for the men and women she meets who have committed horrible murders, she says, "They are more than the worst thing they've ever done. There's always the capacity to be more than we have been and for God's grace to change us."

"Human beings do unspeakable acts, and I am outraged over those acts. But when you meet the real person and you meet a human being, you know you're not meeting a monster," she says. You're meeting a person with a story. It's a story that most often involves them being wounded as a child or abused and they are often poor. "Ninety percent of people on death row were abused as children and had violence pumped into them. One day they pumped out violence on other people," she says.[1] Race also unfairly influences imposition of the death penalty since most of those on death row have murdered a white person. Murders of people of color aren't treated the same way.

In her ministry, Sr. Helen holds in her soul the outrage she feels over the death of the victims and the suffering of the families of both the victims and the perpetrators. She holds in her outrage that a human being who is rendered defenseless in prison is stripped of one's humanity, walked to a death chamber, and killed. "It's easy to kill a monster," she has told many crowds. "If you look into the face of a human being who did unspeakable crimes, it is very different to kill them."[2]

People in prison are often victimized by a broken legal system. A district attorney can only ask for the death penalty if there is an eyewitness who says he or she saw the other person commit the crime. What if that eyewitness is offered a lesser sentence to lie in implicating the other person? How do we know from square one that we have the truth? Only the worst of the worst are supposed to be executed in America. How do we determine that, Sr. Helen asks.

Often an ambitious district attorney or other elected officials will hide evidence or manipulate the system to get the outcome that benefits their careers the most, which can be getting a death penalty sentence for someone. They should be held accountable for such things, Sr. Helen believes. They are protected from that retribution and given immunity. Immunity is understandable when people are looking for revenge, but not when they have deliberately done wrong. The fact that one person's personal motivation can influence whether or not death enters into a sentence shows that the death penalty is applied differently depending upon the county or state. How can that be fair, Sr. Helen often asks.

In *The Death of Innocents*, she wrote, "I've heard criminal defense attorney Millard Farmer (who represented Pat Sonnier at the end) say many times that death penalty cases are 95 percent about politics and 5 percent about criminal justice."[3]

The death penalty is a mostly southern phenomenon practiced by southern states that practiced slavery the longest in the United States. It's an "impossible situation," Sr. Helen says. If federal courts ruled it unconstitutional, it would stop.

"That brings us to a fundamental question about the whole prison system: Is it about punishing people and imposing pain on them, even death, or is it about helping people to change their lives so that they can be citizens again?" Sr. Helen asks. Of course some people should never be put back out into society. "Some of them are sociopaths— there's something wrong with the wiring in their brain and we have to protect ourselves from them. But most human beings who make mistakes, that is not who they are." She dreams of a time when prisons are places where people are rehabilitated and could become good citizens. "That's a fundamental shift to move away from pain and punishment to restoring human life."[4]

Our society often turns to violence as the first response to any situation. Catholics and other people of faith get caught up in that too. But support for the death penalty has steadily declined over the years. Sister Helen sees hope in the younger generations who have shown they support capital punishment less than previous generations. Innocence projects at universities, where students volunteer their time investigating cases, saved many of those exonerated in recent years.

For Sr. Helen, capital punishment is also about human rights. The United Nations adopted the Universal Declaration of Human Rights in 1948, which affirms that all human beings, wherever they are, have a basic dignity and worth. Nowhere in that declaration does it say "except in cases of prisoners or capital punishment." Every time the United

States executes someone it violates that declaration, Sr. Helen believes.

She also feels it violates the UN Convention against Torture. "I have met people, some on death row who couldn't take the mental strain of it. They were watching other people be led to execution. They would get close to execution and they just gave up all their appeals and said 'Let the state kill me,' which is a way of committing suicide when you let the state help you do that," Sr. Helen says. "Can you imagine the tension? You're in a six-and-a-half by eight-and-a-half-foot cell, twenty-three out of twenty-four hours of every day waiting to be killed. One day I am hopeful that we will crack open that this is in fact an act of torture. We have signed on to the UN Convention against Torture, and it defines torture as an extreme mental or physical assault on someone rendered defenseless."[5]

Some people tell her they would rather be dead than in prison. While bad things like rapes and fights do happen in prison, there is opportunity to live a life. We have a picture in our minds that prisons are so terrible, like in the story of *Dead Man Walking*. Pat Sonnier was executed, but his brother Eddie Sonnier got two life sentences. He was never going to walk out of prison alive, but he made his way, Sr. Helen says. "He had a job in the welding shop. He made friends. He got an education. He read books. He had a life. You can find that when you're alive you have a life."[6]

To those in support of the death penalty, Sr. Helen asks who should kill those who are condemned. Would you pull the switch? Would you want your brother, your child, or your mother to be the one to do the killing? How would that affect them?

That is a sentiment shared by many of the people involved in executions. In *Dead Man Walking*, she wrote about a conversation with Major Kendall Coody, the supervisor of death row at the Louisiana State Penitentiary at the time she was visiting Robert Lee Willie. She described him as a troubled man: "I'm not sure how long I'm going to be able to keep doing this," he says. "I've been through five of these executions and I can't eat, I can't sleep. I'm dreaming about executions. I don't condone these guys' crimes. I know they've done terrible things. I don't excuse what they've done, but I talk to them when I make my rounds. I talk to them and many of them are just little boys inside big men's bodies, little boys who never had much chance to grow up."[7]

Coody also was part of the group who walked the prisoner to the electric chair. The effects of killing someone reach far beyond just the condemned and the victims' families. In recent years, more guards, wardens, and other prison staff involved in executions are speaking out about it.

Ron McAndrews was a warden at Florida State Prison from 1996 to 1998 and oversaw three executions. When the third one went wrong, it changed his life. He describes what happened in a 2014 essay in *Esquire*:

> My last electrocution at Florida State Prison was the Pedro Medina execution. Pedro was an inmate I really got to know before his death. I read all his files, the pre-sentence investigation, all the documents.
>
> This was my third execution. As I told the executioner to turn on the electricity, there was a pop. Immediately following the pop, there was a plume of smoke that came from beneath the helmet, sort of out in front of my face, with a bad odor. Then there was a long flame. It was a flame that dipped down out of the helmet and in front of my face. It almost hit me. The flame was so long. I was standing two and a half, three feet away from the electric chair. I couldn't believe it. For the next eleven minutes,

instead of electrocuting this man, we burned him to death. We literally burned him to death. I'll never forget the muscles in his body, the twisting, the clenching of his fists, his toes turning apart like they were being pried apart by a wrench. It was the most ghastly thing I've ever seen, and I've seen a lot of dead people in my time.[8]

While McAndrews always had difficulty sleeping since he became warden, soon he started to have nightmares seeing the faces of those he killed. It was getting to him, and he was self-medicating with pills and alcohol. Soon he quit his job. He eventually got better but didn't find peace until he admitted the death penalty was wrong and he should do something about it.

The American people are good people, Sr. Helen believes. It is just that they have never reflected deeply on the issue of the death penalty. If they did they would never condone it. Until they do—or as long as she has breath—Sr. Helen will continue to share with people what God had her witness on that fateful day in Angola Prison, April 5, 1984.

Notes

Chapter Two:
Her Early Years—pages 5–22

    1. Conversation with the author, December 9, 2015.

    2. Ibid.

    3. Ibid.

    4. Conversation with the author, June 11, 2016.

    5. Ibid.

    6. Eileen Mitchell, "Called to Inclusive Love: CSJ Charism, Spirituality, Mission," *Sisters of St. Joseph Associate Formation Guide,* Congregation of St. Joseph (2011).

    7. Conversation with the author, December 9, 2015.

    8. Ibid.

    9. Ibid.

    10. Ibid.

    11. Conversation with the author, June 11, 2016.

    12. Conversation with the author, June 24, 2016.

    13. Ibid.

    14. Helen Prejean, *Dead Man Walking: An Eyewitness Account of the Death Penalty in the United States* (New York: Random House, 1993), 10.

Chapter Three:
Patrick Sonnier—pages 23–36

    1. Conversation with the author, December 9, 2015.

    2. Ibid.

3. Prejean, *Dead Man Walking*, 13.
4. Ibid., 14.
5. Conversation with the author, December 9, 2015.
6. Prejean, *Dead Man Walking*, 28.
7. Helen Prejean Papers, Box 001, Folder 007, DePaul University Special Collections and Archives, Chicago, IL.
8. Ibid.
9. Prejean, *Dead Man Walking*, 37.
10. Ibid., 38.
11. Prejean Papers, Folder 009.
12. Ibid.
13. Ibid., Folder 010.
14. Ibid.
15. Ibid., Folder 006.
16. Ibid.
17. Ibid.
18. Ibid., Folder 005.
19. Prejean, *Dead Man Walking*, 76.
20. Ibid., 99.
21. Conversation with the author, December 9, 2015.
22. Ibid.

Chapter Four:
Dead Man Walking—pages 37–53

1. Conversation with the author, December 9, 2015.
2. Qtd. in Sue Halpern, "Sister Sympathy," *New York Times Magazine*, May 9, 1993: http://www.nytimes.com/1993/05/09/magazine/sister-sympathy.html.
3. Conversation with the author, June 11, 2016.
4. Halpern, "Sister Sympathy."
5. Conversation with the author, June 11, 2016.
6. Ibid.
7. Laura Shapiro, "I Would Not Want My Murderer Executed," *New York Times*, July 4, 1993.
8. Halpern, "Sister Sympathy."

9. John Feister, "The Real Woman behind *Dead Man Walking*," *St. Anthony Messenger*, April 1996.

10. Ibid.

11. Roger Ebert, review of *Dead Man Walking* (film), dir. Tim Robbins, *Chicago Sun-Times*, January 12, 1996, www.rogerebert .com/reviews/dead-man-walking-1996.

12. "Susan Sarandon winning Best Actress," YouTube video, 4:34, from the 68th Academy Awards ceremony on March 25, 1996, posted by "Oscars," May 14, 2008, www.youtube.com/watch?v=JeQdw QLwYUU.

13. The Actor's Gang, http://www.theactorsgang.com.

14. Kate Bissell, "Actor's Gang: How Tim Robbins has cut reoffending rates," *BBC News Magazine*, March 14, 2016, http://www .bbc.com/news/magazine-35786775.

15. Prejean, *Dead Man Walking*, 64.

16. Conversation with the author, December 9, 2015.

17. Ibid.

18. Prejean, *Dead Man Walking*, 65.

19. USCCB Committee on Domestic Policy, *A Culture of Life and the Penalty of Death* (Washington, DC: USCCB, 2005), 16, http:// www.usccb.org/_cs_upload/7917_1.pdf.

20. Ibid., 20.

21. Conversation with the author, December 9, 2015.

Chapter Five:
The Death of Innocents—pages 54–68

1. Helen Prejean, *The Death of Innocents: An Eyewitness Account of Wrongful Executions* (New York: Vintage, 2005), 4.

2. Prejean Papers, Box 005, Folder 005.

3. Ibid.

4. Ibid., Folder 006.

5. Ibid., Folder 005.

6. Ibid., Folder 004.

7. Ibid.

8. Ibid.

9. Prejean, *Death of Innocents,* 45.

10. Ibid., 50.

11. Prejean Papers, Box 007, Folder 008.

12. Prejean, *Death of Innocents,* 9.

13. Ibid., 58.

14. Conversation with the author, December 9, 2015.

15. Prejean, *Death of Innocents,* 84.

16. Ibid., 75.

17. Ibid., 278.

18. Ibid., 149.

19. Ibid., 154.

20. Ibid., 157.

21. Ibid., 162.

22. Ibid., 163.

Chapter Six:
The Church and the Death Penalty—pages 69–83

1. Conversation with the author, December 9, 2015.

2. Saint John Paul II, Encyclical on the Value and Inviolability of Human Life (*Evangelium Vitae*), March 25, 1995, 56, http://w2 .vatican.va/content/john-paul-ii/en/encyclicals/documents/hf_jp-ii_ enc_25031995_evangelium-vitae.html.

3. Prejean, *The Death of Innocents,* 126.

4. Ibid., 124.

5. Ibid., 126.

6. Ibid., 127.

7. Ibid.

8. Conversation with the author, December 9, 2015.

9. *Catechism of the Catholic Church,* 2nd ed., (Vatican City: Libreria Editrice Vaticana, 1997), 2267.

10. John Paul II, Homily at Trans World Dome in St. Louis, MO, January 27, 1999, http://w2.vatican.va/content/john-paul-ii/en /travels/1999/documents/hf_jp-ii_hom_27011999_stlouis.html.

11. USCCB, "Bishops' Statement on Capital Punishment, 1980," http://www.usccb.org/issues-and-action/human-life-and-dignity/death -penalty-capital-punishment/statement-on-capital-punishment.cfm.

12. Ibid.

13. USCCB Committee on Domestic Policy, *A Culture of Life and the Penalty of Death*, 14–15.

14. Pope Francis, Address to the Joint Session of the United States Congress, Washington, DC, September 24, 2015, http://w2.vatican.va/content/francesco/en/speeches/2015/september/documents/papa-francesco_20150924_usa-us-congress.html.

15. Conversation with the author, December 9, 2015.

16. Glossip v. Gross, 576 U.S. ___ (2015), http://www.supremecourt.gov/opinions/14pdf/14-7955_aplc.pdf.

17. Conversation with the author, December 9, 2015.

18. Ibid.

19. Ibid.

Chapter Seven:
Her Thoughts on the Death Penalty—pages 84–89

1. Conversation with the author, December 9, 2015.

2. Helen Prejean, speaking to students at St. Catherine–St. Lucy School, Oak Park, IL, October 17, 2015.

3. Prejean, *The Death of Innocents*, 103.

4. Conversation with the author, December 9, 2015.

5. Ibid.

6. Ibid.

7. Prejean, *Dead Man Walking*, 180.

8. Ron McAndrew, "Ron McAndrew Is Done Killing People," *Esquire*, (January 14, 2014), http://www.esquire.com/news-politics/news/a26833/ron-mcandrew-is-done-killing-people/.

Bibliography

Bissell, Kate. "Actor's Gang: How Tim Robbins has cut reoffending rates." *BBC News Magazine*, March 14, 2016.

Ebert, Roger. Review of *Dead Man Walking* (film), directed by Tim Robbins. *Chicago Sun-Times*, January 12, 1996.

Feister, John. "The Real Woman behind *Dead Man Walking*," *St. Anthony Messenger*, April 1996.

Francis, Pope. Address to the Joint Session of the United States Congress, Washington, DC, September 24, 2015.

John Paul II, Saint. Encyclical on the Value and Inviolability of Human Life (*Evangelium Vitae*), March 25, 1995.

———. Homily at Trans World Dome, St. Louis, MO, January 27, 1999.

McAndrew, Ron. "Ron McAndrew Is Done Killing People." *Esquire,* January 14, 2014.

Mitchell, Eileen. "Called to Inclusive Love: CSJ Charism, Spirituality, Mission." *Sisters of St. Joseph Associate Formation Guide,* Congregation of St. Joseph (2011).

Prejean, Helen. *Dead Man Walking: An Eyewitness Account of the Death Penalty in the United States*. New York: Random House, 1993.

———. *The Death of Innocents: An Eyewitness Account of Wrongful Executions*. New York: Vintage, 2005.

———. Papers. DePaul University Special Collections and Archives, Chicago, IL.

Shapiro, Laura. "I Would Not Want My Murderer Executed." *New York Times*, July 4, 1993.

USCCB Committee on Domestic Policy. *A Culture of Life and the Penalty of Death*. Washington, DC: USCCB, 2005. http://www.usccb.org/_cs_upload/7917_1.pdf.

United States Conference of Catholic Bishops. "Bishops' Statement on Capital Punishment, 1980." Washington, DC: USCCB, 1980.

———. Committee on Domestic Policy. *A Culture of Life and the Penalty of Death*. Washington, DC: USCCB, 2005.

Interviews

Prejean, Helen. Conversation with the author, December 9, 2015.

———. Conversation with the author, June 11, 2016

———. Conversation with the author, June 24, 2016

Index